D0411999
150
BAKING
recipes
150
CAKE
recipes
150
CHICKEN
recipes
150
CUPCAKE
& MUFFIN
recipes
150
FAST
& SIMPLE
recipes
150
INDIAN
recipes
150
PASTA
recipes
150
SLOW
COOKER
recipes
150
STIR-FRY
recipes
150
STUDENT
recipes
150
TAPAS
recipes
150
VEGETARIAN
recipes

CHICKEN
recipes

INSPIRED IDEAS FOR
EVERYDAY COOKING

CONTENTS

INTRODUCTION 4

SOUPS & SALADS 6

QUICK & EASY 56

FAMILY MEALS 106

WINTER WARMERS 156

AROUND THE WORLD 206

INDEX 254

INTRODUCTION

Chicken is very popular and versatile and it can be used to create a vast array of delicious dishes. It is readily available and can also be an economical choice, depending on the type you buy and whether you buy a whole bird or chicken portions/pieces.

We include an inspiring selection of tempting chicken dishes from across the world to suit all tastes, with recipes that will appeal to adults, children and teenagers alike.

As well as being an excellent source of protein, chicken provides some vitamins and minerals, including B vitamins and selenium. Chicken is low in fat and is lower in saturated fat than many other meats, especially when the skin is removed.

We kick things off with some sensational soups and salads, including classics such as Cream of Chicken Soup and Chicken Noodle Soup, as well as others ideal for warming wintry days, such as Chicken & Barley Broth. Colourful and nutritious salads bursting with feel-good vitamins and minerals include Warm Chicken & Mango Salad and Chicken Caesar Salad.

A collection of quick and easy chicken delights includes popular favourites such as Chicken-Loaded Potato Skins, Chicken Satay Skewers and Chicken Fajitas. Fantastic family favourites, ideal for gathering everyone around the table, include Roast Chicken, Individual Chicken Pies and The Ultimate Chicken Burger.

Wonderful winter warmers feature a tempting range of comforting casseroles such as Hunter's Chicken and Chicken, Pumpkin & Chorizo Casserole, or try spicing things up a bit for the more adventurous appetites with Cajun Chicken and Spicy Aromatic Chicken.

Finally, take inspiration from our marvellous medley of chicken dishes from around the world and transport your taste buds to all corners of the globe by creating temptations such as Chicken Tagine, Green Chicken Curry and Jambalaya.

Chicken is versatile and can be cooked in a wide variety of ways, including roasting, baking, frying, stir-frying, grilling, griddling, poaching, steaming, casseroling and braising. Fresh or frozen raw chicken is readily available, sold either as whole, oven-ready birds or as a range of chicken portions. Most supermarkets and butchers, as well as some farm shops and farmers' markets, offer a good choice of chicken for purchase. Ideally, buy the best quality chicken that you can afford and choose free-range or organic birds if you can, as they will have had a better upbringing to higher welfare standards and their flavour is often superior.

Wash your hands thoroughly before and after handling raw or cooked chicken, and make sure work surfaces and utensils are cleaned with hot soapy water. Disinfect worktops after use with an antibacterial cleaner.

Always make sure the chicken is thoroughly and evenly cooked before serving and ensure there are no signs of pinkness when you cut into the thickest part of the meat. If the juices are pink or there are traces of blood, continue cooking until the juices run clear. If you are roasting a whole bird, cook until the chicken is tender and the juices run clear when a skewer or fork is inserted into the thickest part of the meat.

Store leftover cooked chicken in a covered or airtight container in the refrigerator and use within 1–2 days. If you are reheating cooked chicken or reheating a dish containing chicken, make sure it is reheated thoroughly and is piping hot throughout before serving. Cooked chicken can be frozen for up to 2 months.

Store fresh chicken loosely covered in a shallow dish in the refrigerator for up to 2 days or according to the 'use-by' date on the label. Ideally, chicken livers and minced chicken should be used within 24 hours of purchase. Fresh raw chicken should be frozen on the day of purchase for up to 3 months.

SOUPS & SALADS

CREAM OF CHICKEN SOUP 8
CHICKEN NOODLE SOUP 10
CHICKEN RAVIOLI IN TARRAGON BROTH 12
CHICKEN & LENTIL SOUP 14
CHICKEN & MUSHROOM SOUP WITH PUFF PASTRY 16
CHICKEN CORN CHOWDER 18
ITALIAN CHICKEN SOUP 19
CHICKEN, AVOCADO & CHIPOTLE SOUP 20
CHICKEN RAMEN 22
CHICKEN & LEMON SOUP 24
CHILLI CHICKEN SOUP 26
CHICKEN TORTILLA SOUP 28
CURRIED CHICKEN SOUP 29
CHICKEN & BEAN SOUP 30
CHICKEN & BARLEY BROTH 31
CHICKEN & THYME SOUP 32
PASTA & CHICKEN MEDLEY 34
COBB SALAD 36
WARM CHICKEN & MANGO SALAD 38
CHICKEN & PESTO SALAD 40
CHICKEN, BACON & AVOCADO SALAD 42
HONEY & CHICKEN PASTA SALAD 44
CURRIED CHICKEN SALAD 46
CHICKEN SALAD CUPS 47
CHICKEN WALDORF SALAD 48
RED CHICKEN SALAD 50
SMOKED CHICKEN & CRANBERRY SALAD 52
CHICKEN CAESAR SALAD 54

CREAM OF CHICKEN SOUP

Serves: 4

Prep: 15 mins, plus cooling

Cook: 45 mins

Ingredients

- 3 tbsp butter
- 4 shallots, chopped
- 1 leek, sliced
- 450 g/1 lb skinless, boneless chicken breasts, chopped
- 600 ml/1 pint chicken stock
- 1 tbsp chopped fresh parsley
- 1 tbsp chopped fresh thyme, plus extra sprigs to garnish
- 175 ml/6 fl oz double cream
- salt and pepper

Method

1. Melt the butter in a large saucepan over a medium heat. Add the shallots and cook, stirring, for 3 minutes, until slightly softened.
2. Add the leek and cook for a further 5 minutes, stirring.
3. Add the chicken, stock and herbs, and season to taste with salt and pepper. Bring to the boil, then reduce the heat and simmer for 25 minutes, until the chicken is tender and cooked through.
4. Remove from the heat and leave to cool for 10 minutes. Transfer the soup to a food processor or blender and process until smooth (you may need to do this in batches).
5. Return the soup to the rinsed-out pan and warm over a low heat for 5 minutes.
6. Stir in the cream and cook for a further 2 minutes, then remove from the heat and ladle into warmed serving bowls. Garnish with thyme sprigs and serve immediately.

★ Variation

For a lower-fat version of this soup omit the double cream but replace half the chicken stock with semi-skimmed milk.

CHICKEN NOODLE SOUP

Serves: 6 **Prep: 15 mins** **Cook: 45–55 mins**

Ingredients

- 175 g/6 oz egg noodles
- 2 tbsp olive oil
- 8 spring onions, chopped
- 4 bacon rashers, chopped
- 2 tsp chopped fresh tarragon
- 6 skinless boneless chicken thighs, diced
- 150 ml/5 fl oz dry white wine
- 1.2 litres/2 pints basic vegetable stock
- salt and pepper
- crusty bread, to serve

Method

1. Bring a saucepan of water to the boil. Add the noodles and cook according to the instructions on the packet. Drain, refresh under cold running water and leave to stand in a bowl of water.
2. Heat the oil in a large saucepan. Add the spring onions and bacon and cook over a low heat, stirring occasionally, for 5 minutes, until the spring onions have softened and the bacon is beginning to colour.
3. Add the tarragon and chicken, increase the heat to medium and cook, stirring frequently, for about 8 minutes, until the chicken is golden brown all over.
4. Pour in the wine and cook for 2 minutes, until the alcohol has evaporated, then pour in enough of the stock just to cover the meat. Reduce the heat, cover and simmer for 20–30 minutes, until the chicken is tender and cooked through.
5. Pour in the remaining stock, season with salt and pepper and bring to the boil. Drain the noodles and add to the pan, heat through briefly. Ladle the soup into warmed bowls and serve immediately with crusty bread.

CHICKEN RAVIOLI IN TARRAGON BROTH

Serves: 6

Prep: 50 mins, plus chilling & drying

Cook: 35–40 mins

Ingredients

2 litres/3½ pints chicken stock

2 tbsp finely chopped fresh tarragon leaves

freshly grated Parmesan cheese, to serve

Pasta dough

125 g/4½ oz flour, plus extra if needed

2 tbsp fresh tarragon leaves, stems removed

1 egg

1 egg, separated

1 tsp extra virgin olive oil

2–3 tbsp water

pinch of salt

Filling

200 g/7 oz skinless, boneless cooked chicken, coarsely chopped

½ tsp grated lemon rind

2 tbsp chopped mixed fresh tarragon, chives and parsley

4 tbsp whipping cream

salt and pepper

Method

1. To make the pasta, combine the flour, tarragon and salt in a food processor or blender. Beat together the egg, egg yolk, oil and 2 tablespoons of water. With the machine running, pour in the egg mixture and process until it forms a ball (use a further tablespoon of water if needed). Wrap and chill for 30 minutes. Reserve the egg white.
2. To make the filling, put the chicken, lemon rind and mixed herbs in a food processor or blender and season to taste with salt and pepper. Chop finely. Do not overprocess. Scrape into a bowl and stir in the cream.
3. Divide the pasta dough in half. Cover one half and roll out the other half on a floured surface to less than 1.5 mm/1⁄16 inch. Cut out rectangles measuring about 10 x 5 cm/4 x 2 inches. Place a teaspoon of filling on one half of each rectangle. Brush the edges with egg white and fold in half. Press the edge to seal. Arrange on a baking sheet dusted with flour. Repeat with the remaining dough. Allow the ravioli to dry for about 15 minutes or chill for 1–2 hours.
4. Bring a large pan of water to the boil. Drop in half of the ravioli and cook for 12–15 minutes, or until just tender and the filling is piping hot. Drain on a tea towel while cooking the remainder.

5 Meanwhile, put the stock and tarragon in a large pan. Bring to the boil, then cover and simmer for 15 minutes. Add the ravioli and simmer for a further 5 minutes. Ladle into warmed bowls and serve immediately with Parmesan cheese.

CHICKEN & LENTIL SOUP

Serves: 6 **Prep: 15 mins** **Cook: 1 hour 25 mins–1 hour 35 mins**

Ingredients

- 3 tbsp olive oil
- 1 large onion, chopped
- 2 leeks, chopped
- 2 carrots, chopped
- 2 sticks celery, chopped
- 175 g/6 oz button mushrooms, chopped
- 4 tbsp dry white wine
- 1.2 litres/2 pints vegetable stock
- 1 bay leaf
- 2 tsp dried mixed herbs
- 175 g/6 oz Puy lentils
- 350 g/12 oz skinless, boneless cooked chicken, diced
- salt and pepper

Method

1. Heat the oil in a large saucepan. Add the onion, leeks, carrots, celery and mushrooms and cook over a low heat, stirring occasionally, for 5–7 minutes, until softened but not coloured.
2. Increase the heat to medium, pour in the wine and cook for 2–3 minutes, until the alcohol has evaporated, then pour in the stock.
3. Bring to the boil, add the bay leaf and herbs, reduce the heat, cover and simmer for 30 minutes. Add the lentils, re-cover the pan and simmer, stirring occasionally, for a further 40 minutes, until they are tender.
4. Stir in the chicken, season to taste with salt and pepper and simmer for a further 5–10 minutes, until the chicken is piping hot. Remove and discard the bay leaf and serve immediately.

2
3
3

CHICKEN & MUSHROOM SOUP WITH PUFF PASTRY

Serves: 4

Prep: 25 mins, plus cooling

Cook: 1 hour–5 mins

Ingredients

- 2 skinless chicken legs
- 1 litre/1¾ pints chicken stock
- 150 ml/5 fl oz dry cider
- 1 onion, finely chopped
- 1 bay leaf
- 250 g/9 oz chestnut mushrooms, thickly sliced
- 4 tbsp cornflour blended with 4 tbsp water
- 4 tbsp crème fraîche
- flour for sprinkling
- 500 g/1 lb 2 oz ready-made puff pastry
- salt and pepper

Method

1. Place the chicken legs in a large saucepan with the stock, cider, onion and bay leaf. Cover and simmer for 25 minutes until the chicken is cooked through and the juices run clear when a skewer is inserted into the thickest part of the meat. Add the mushrooms and simmer for a further 10 minutes. Remove the chicken and set aside. Remove and discard the bay leaf.
2. Stir the cornflour into the stock. Heat, stirring constantly, until boiling and thickened. Remove from the heat and leave to cool. Remove the meat from the chicken legs and tear into pieces.
3. Preheat the oven to 200°C/400°F/Gas Mark 6. Stir the chicken and crème fraîche into the soup. Season to taste with salt and pepper then ladle into ovenproof bowls. They should be about three quarters full.
4. Lightly flour a surface, then roll out the pastry. Cut out rounds or squares large enough to cover the tops of the bowls with a 1 cm/½ inch overlap. Brush the rim of each bowl with water, lay the pastry on top, press around the rim and pierce the centres. Bake in the preheated oven for 20–25 minutes, or until the pastry is golden. Serve immediately.

2
4

CHICKEN SWEETCORN CHOWDER

Serves: 8 **Prep: 15 mins** **Cook: 45–50 mins**

Ingredients

3 bacon rashers, diced
1 large onion, diced
1 carrot, diced
1 celery stick, diced
1 green pepper, diced
450 g/1 lb red potatoes, peeled and cut into 5-mm/¼-inch cubes
450 g/1 lb skinless, boneless chicken breast, diced
1.5 litres/2¾ pints chicken stock
2 fresh thyme sprigs
450 g/1 lb fresh or frozen sweetcorn kernels
350 ml/12 fl oz double cream
salt and pepper

Method

1 Cook the bacon in a large saucepan over a medium heat, stirring, until crisp. Use a slotted spoon to transfer the bacon to a plate lined with kitchen paper and reserve. Add the onion, carrot, celery and green pepper to the bacon fat in the pan and cook for about 10 minutes, stirring, until the onion is translucent.

2 Add the potatoes, chicken, stock, thyme, sweetcorn and a large pinch of salt. Simmer, covered, over a medium–low heat until the potatoes are tender and the chicken is cooked through. Add the cream, stir and cook, uncovered, for 12 minutes. Season to taste with salt and pepper. Serve in warmed bowls with the bacon sprinkled over the top.

ITALIAN CHICKEN SOUP

Serves: 4 **Prep: 15 mins** **Cook: 15 mins**

Ingredients

- 450 g/1 lb skinless, boneless chicken breasts, cut into thin strips
- 1.2 litres/2 pints chicken stock
- 150 ml/5 fl oz double cream
- 115 g/4 oz dried vermicelli
- 1 tbsp cornflour
- 3 tbsp milk
- 175 g/6 oz canned sweetcorn kernels, drained
- salt and pepper
- basil leaf, to garnish

Method

1. Place the chicken in a large saucepan and pour in the chicken stock and cream. Bring to the boil, then reduce the heat and simmer for 20 minutes until the chicken is cooked through.
2. Meanwhile, bring a large saucepan of lightly salted water to the boil. Add the pasta, bring back to the boil and cook for 8–10 minutes, until tender but still firm to the bite. Drain thoroughly and keep warm.
3. Mix the cornflour and milk together until a smooth paste forms, then stir it into the soup. Season to taste with salt and pepper, add the sweetcorn and pasta and heat through. Ladle the soup into warmed soup bowls, garnish with a basil leaf and serve immediately.

CHICKEN, AVOCADO & CHIPOTLE SOUP

Serves: 6 **Prep: 15 mins** **Cook: 5 mins**

Ingredients

1.5 litres/2¾ pints chicken stock

2–3 cloves garlic, finely chopped

1–2 dried chipotle chillies, thinly sliced

1 avocado

juice of ½ lime

3–5 spring onions, thinly sliced

400 g/14 oz skinless, boneless cooked chicken breast, torn into bite-sized pieces

2 tbsp chopped fresh coriander

1 lime, cut into wedges, to serve

Method

1 Place the stock in a large saucepan with the garlic and chillies and bring to the boil.

2 Meanwhile, cut the avocado in half around the stone. Twist apart, then remove the stone with a knife. Remove and discard the skin, dice the flesh and toss in the lime juice to prevent discoloration.

3 Arrange the spring onions, chicken, avocado and coriander in warmed bowls.

4 Ladle hot stock over and serve immediately with lime wedges.

CHICKEN RAMEN

Serves: 4

Prep: 20 mins, plus cooling

Cook: 45 mins

Ingredients

850 ml/1½ pints chicken stock

2 skinless, boneless chicken breasts

3 spring onions, sliced into 5-cm/2-inch pieces

4-cm/1½-inch piece fresh ginger, thickly sliced

1 tbsp soy sauce

85 g/3 oz ramen noodles

115 g/4 oz baby spinach

4 baby corn cobs, diagonally sliced into 3 pieces

60 g/2¼ oz mung beansprouts

salt and pepper

Method

1. Pour 600 ml/1 pint of the stock into a wok with a lid. Add the chicken, spring onions, ginger and soy sauce. Slowly bring to the boil, skimming off any foam. Reduce the heat, cover and simmer gently for 30 minutes, until the chicken is cooked through and the juices run clear when a skewer is inserted into the thickest part of the meat.
2. Pour the contents of the wok into a large bowl and leave the chicken to cool slightly in the liquid. Remove the chicken from the liquid and slice into thin pieces. Set aside and keep warm.
3. Strain the liquid through a sieve, discarding the spring onions and ginger. Wipe the wok clean with kitchen paper, then pour in the strained liquid and the remaining stock. Bring to the boil, then add the noodles and cook for 3–4 minutes, until tender but still firm to the bite. Use tongs to remove the noodles from the wok and divide them between four warmed soup bowls.
4. Bring the liquid in the wok back to the boil. Add the spinach and corn and cook for 1 minute, or until the spinach is wilted. Add the beansprouts and cook for a further few seconds.
5. Season to taste. Divide the chicken between the soup bowls, then pour over the hot stock and vegetables. Serve immediately.

1
3
4

CHICKEN & LEMON SOUP

Serves: 4 **Prep: 20 mins** **Cook: 45–50 mins**

Ingredients

- 4 tbsp butter
- 8 shallots, thinly sliced
- 2 carrots, thinly sliced
- 2 sticks celery, thinly sliced
- 225 g/8 oz skinless, boneless chicken breasts, finely chopped
- 3 lemons
- 1.2 litres/2 pints chicken stock
- 225 g/8 oz dried spaghetti, broken into small pieces
- 150 ml/5 fl oz double cream
- salt and pepper
- 2 lemon slices, halved, to garnish

Method

1. Melt the butter in a large saucepan. Add the shallots, carrots, celery and chicken and cook over a low heat, stirring occasionally, for 5 minutes.
2. Thinly pare the lemons and blanch the lemon rind in boiling water for 3 minutes. Squeeze the juice from the lemon and reserve.
3. Add the lemon rind and juice to the saucepan, together with the stock. Bring the soup to the boil, then reduce the heat and simmer for 40 minutes, stirring occasionally.
4. Add the spaghetti to the saucepan and cook for 15 minutes, or until the spaghetti is tender and the chicken is cooked through. Season to taste with salt and pepper and add the cream. Heat through gently; do not allow the soup to boil.
5. Ladle into warmed bowls, garnish with slices of lemon and serve immediately.

CHILLI CHICKEN SOUP

Serves: 4 **Prep: 15 mins** **Cook: 30 mins**

Ingredients

1 tbsp vegetable oil

1 onion, finely chopped

2 sticks celery, finely chopped

2 carrots, finely chopped

1 red chilli, deseeded and finely chopped

2 cloves garlic, crushed

2 tbsp tomato purée

1 tbsp fresh oregano, finely chopped

600 g/1 lb 5 oz canned whole tomatoes, drained

500 ml/18 fl oz chicken stock

375 g/13 oz skinless boneless chicken breasts, diced

juice of 1 lime

salt and pepper

To garnish

tortilla chips, broken into pieces

½ avocado, peeled, stoned and finely chopped

4 tsp chopped fresh coriander

Method

1. Heat the oil in a large saucepan and sauté the onion, celery, carrots, chilli and garlic and cook for 4–5 minutes.
2. Add the tomato purée and cook for a further 1 minute, stirring constantly.
3. Add the oregano, tomatoes and stock and bring to a gentle simmer, breaking down the tomatoes with the back of a wooden spoon to release the juices.
4. Add the chicken and season to taste with salt and pepper, cover and cook for a further 20 minutes until the chicken is tender and cooked through.
5. Remove from the heat, stir in the lime juice and ladle the soup into warmed serving bowls. Serve each portion topped with a selection of garnishes.

1
3
5

CHICKEN TORTILLA SOUP

Serves: 4 **Prep: 20 mins** **Cook: 30 mins**

Ingredients

1 tbsp vegetable oil
1 onion, chopped
2 garlic cloves, finely chopped
2 skinless, boneless chicken breasts, diced
1.5 litres/2¾ pints chicken stock
175 g/6 oz tomatoes, diced
juice of 1 lemon
½ tsp chilli powder
¼ tsp ground cumin
⅛ tsp chipotle chilli powder
1 avocado, peeled, stoned and cubed
2 tbsp chopped fresh coriander
200 g/7 oz tortilla chips, broken
55 g/2 oz Cheddar cheese, coarsely grated

Method

1 Place a large saucepan over a medium heat, add the oil, onion and garlic and cook for 3 minutes. Add the chicken, stock, tomatoes, lemon juice, chilli powder, cumin and chipotle chilli powder.

2 Heat until simmering, then reduce the heat to low and cook for a further 20 minutes until the chicken is tender and cooked through. Remove from the heat and stir in the avocado and coriander. Divide the tortilla chips between four warmed bowls and pour over the soup. Top with the cheese and serve immediately.

CURRIED CHICKEN SOUP

Serves: 6

Prep: 20 mins, plus cooling

Cook: 1 hour 5 mins

Ingredients

55 g/2 oz butter

2 onions, chopped

1 small turnip, cut into small dice

2 carrots, finely sliced

1 eating apple, cored, peeled and chopped

2 tbsp mild curry powder

1.2 litres/2 pints chicken stock

juice of ½ lemon

175 g/6 oz skinless, boneless cooked chicken, diced

2 tbsp chopped fresh coriander, plus extra to garnish

salt and pepper

55 g/2 oz cooked rice, to serve

Method

1 Melt the butter in a large saucepan over a medium heat, add the onions and sauté gently for 5 minutes, until soft but not brown.

2 Add the turnip, carrots and apple and continue to cook for a further 3–4 minutes.

3 Stir in the curry powder until the vegetables are well coated, then pour in the stock. Bring to the boil, cover and simmer for 45 minutes. Season well with salt and pepper and add the lemon juice.

4 Remove the saucepan from the heat and leave to cool slightly. Transfer to a food processor or blender, in batches if necessary, and process to a purée. Return the soup to the rinsed-out pan, add the chicken and coriander and heat until the chicken is piping hot.

5 Place a spoonful of rice in each serving bowl and pour the soup over the top. Garnish with coriander and serve immediately.

CHICKEN & BEAN SOUP

Serves: 4 **Prep: 15 mins** **Cook: 20 mins**

Ingredients

2 tbsp olive oil

2 skinless, boneless chicken breasts, thinly sliced

2 cloves garlic, crushed

2 courgettes, cut into large dice

200 g/7 oz French beans, cut into 1 cm/½ inch pieces

350 g/12 oz tomatoes, deseeded and roughly chopped

410 g/14½ oz canned pinto beans, drained and rinsed

1.2 litres/2 pints vegetable stock

12 fresh basil leaves, chopped

pepper

Method

1. Heat the oil in a large saucepan set over a medium heat. Add the chicken and garlic and cook, stirring, for 3 minutes. Try not to let the chicken or garlic brown.
2. Stir in the courgettes, beans, tomatoes, pinto beans and stock. Cover and simmer for 10–12 minutes, or until the chicken is cooked through and the vegetables are tender.
3. Stir in the basil leaves and season to taste with pepper. Ladle into warmed bowls and serve immediately.

CHICKEN & BARLEY BROTH

Serves: 6

Prep: 10 mins, plus standing

Cook: 2¾ hours

Ingredients

- 55 g/2 oz pre-soaked dried peas
- 900 g/2 lb skinless, boneless chicken breasts, diced
- 1.2 litres/2 pints chicken stock
- 600 ml/1 pint water
- 55 g/2 oz barley
- 1 large carrot, diced
- 1 small turnip, diced
- 1 large leek, thinly sliced
- 1 red onion, finely chopped
- salt and white pepper
- 1 tbsp chopped fresh parsley, to garnish
- bread, to serve

Method

1. Put the pre-soaked peas and diced chicken into a saucepan, then add the stock and water and bring slowly to the boil. Skim the stock as it boils. Wash the barley thoroughly and set aside.
2. When all the foam is removed, add the washed barley and a pinch of salt and simmer for 35 minutes.
3. Add the rest of the ingredients and simmer for 35 minutes until the chicken is cooked through.
4. Let the broth stand for at least 48 hours. Reheat, adjust the seasoning, garnish with parsley and serve with bread.

CHICKEN & THYME SOUP

Serves: 6

Prep: 15 mins, plus cooling

Cook: 45–50 mins

Ingredients

- 1 tbsp olive oil
- 1 onion, diced
- 4 cloves garlic, finely chopped
- 2 carrots, diced
- 2 sticks celery, diced
- 1.5 litres/2¾ pints chicken stock
- 4 sprigs fresh thyme
- 1 bay leaf
- ½ tsp pepper, plus extra to garnish
- 450 g/1 lb skinless, boneless chicken breasts
- 225 g/8 oz dried pasta
- grated zest and juice of 1 lemon

Method

1. In a large, heavy-based saucepan, heat the oil over a medium–high heat. Add the onion and garlic and sauté, stirring frequently, for about 5 minutes or until soft. Add the carrots and celery and cook for a further 1–2 minutes. Add the stock, thyme, bay leaf and pepper and bring to the boil.
2. Reduce heat to medium–low and add the chicken breasts. Simmer for about 20 minutes until the chicken is cooked through and the juices run clear when a skewer is inserted into the thickest part of the meat. Remove the chicken from the pan and set aside. When cool enough to handle, cut the chicken into bite-sized pieces.
3. Remove the thyme sprigs and bay leaf from the soup and discard them. Return the soup to a simmer over a medium heat.
4. Cook the pasta according to packet instructions and drain. Add the cooked pasta and cooked chicken to the soup and simmer for about 5 minutes or until the chicken is piping hot. Just before serving, stir in the lemon zest and juice. Serve immediately, garnished with freshly ground pepper.

2
4

PASTA & CHICKEN MEDLEY

Serves: 2

Prep: 20 mins, plus cooling

Cook: 15 mins

Ingredients

- 125–150 g/4½–5½ oz dried fusilli
- 2 tbsp mayonnaise
- 2 tsp pesto
- 1 tbsp soured cream or natural fromage frais
- 175 g/6 oz skinless, boneless cooked chicken, thinly sliced
- 1–2 celery sticks, sliced diagonally
- 125 g/4½ oz black grapes, halved and deseeded
- 1 large carrot, cut into strips
- salt and pepper
- celery leaves, to garnish

Dressing

- 1 tbsp white wine vinegar
- 3 tbsp extra virgin olive oil
- salt and pepper

Method

1. To make the dressing, whisk the vinegar and oil together, then season to taste with salt and pepper.
2. Bring a large saucepan of lightly salted water to the boil. Add the pasta, bring back to the boil and cook for 8–10 minutes, until tender but still firm to the bite. Drain thoroughly. Transfer to a bowl and mix in 1 tablespoon of the dressing while hot, then set aside until cold.
3. Combine the mayonnaise, pesto and soured cream in a bowl, and season to taste with salt and pepper.
4. Add the chicken, celery, grapes, carrot and the mayonnaise mixture to the pasta, and toss thoroughly. Check the seasoning, adding more salt and pepper if necessary.
5. Arrange the pasta mixture in a large serving bowl, garnish with the celery leaves and serve immediately with the reserved dressing.

1
3
4

COBB SALAD

Serves: 4

Prep: 25 mins, plus cooling

Cook: 5 mins

Ingredients

- 8 bacon rashers
- 4 large handfuls mixed salad leaves, torn into bite-sized pieces
- 3 hard-boiled eggs, shelled and chopped
- 450 g/1 lb skinless, boneless cooked chicken, diced
- 2 avocados, peeled, stoned and cubed
- 185 g/6½ oz cherry tomatoes, halved
- 115 g/4 oz Roquefort cheese, crumbled
- bread rolls, to serve

Dressing

- ½ tsp Dijon mustard
- 4 tbsp red wine vinegar
- 1 tsp Worcestershire sauce
- 1 garlic clove, crushed into a paste
- ¼ tsp salt
- ¼ tsp pepper
- 6 tbsp olive oil

Method

1. Put the bacon in a frying pan over a medium–high heat and cook until crisp. Drain on kitchen paper. When it is cool enough to handle, crumble and set aside.
2. Make a bed of salad leaves in four shallow bowls. Arrange the eggs, bacon, chicken, avocados, tomatoes and cheese in rows on top of the lettuce, covering the surface completely.
3. To make the dressing, whisk together the mustard, vinegar, Worcestershire sauce, garlic, salt and pepper. Slowly drizzle in the oil, whisking constantly.
4. Drizzle the dressing evenly over the salad, and serve immediately with bread rolls.

WARM CHICKEN & MANGO SALAD

Serves: 4 **Prep: 20 mins** **Cook: 10 mins**

Ingredients

- 1 tbsp groundnut oil
- 600 g/1 lb 5 oz skinless, boneless chicken breasts, chopped
- 280 g/10 oz French beans, trimmed and cut into 2.5-cm/1-inch lengths
- 280 g/10 oz Chinese leaves, finely shredded
- 4 tbsp chopped fresh coriander
- 85 g/3 oz salted peanuts, roasted and finely chopped
- 1 mango, peeled, stoned and diced

Dressing

- 2 tbsp Thai fish sauce
- 1 tbsp clear honey
- 4 tbsp lemon juice
- 1 red chilli, deseeded and finely chopped

Method

1. Heat a wok over a high heat, then add the oil and heat until smoking. Add the chicken and stir-fry for 2 minutes to seal. Add the French beans, reduce the heat, cover and cook, stirring, for a further 5 minutes or until the chicken is tender and cooked through. Keep warm by covering with a lid.
2. To make the dressing, combine the fish sauce, honey, lemon juice and chopped chilli together in a small bowl. Set aside.
3. Toss the Chinese leaves, coriander and chopped peanuts together in a large serving bowl.
4. Add the diced mango, warm chicken and French beans to the serving bowl, then pour over the dressing. Toss to coat and serve immediately.

1
2
3

CHICKEN & PESTO SALAD

Serves: 4

Prep: 20 mins, plus cooling & chilling

Cook: 20–25 mins

Ingredients

- 4 large chicken thighs
- sunflower oil or olive oil, for brushing
- 200 g/7 oz dried fusilli pasta
- 200 g/7 oz fine French beans, chopped
- 300 g/10½ oz ready-made pesto, plus extra if needed
- 2 large tomatoes, sliced
- salt and pepper
- fresh basil leaves, to garnish

Method

1. Preheat the grill to medium–high and position the grill rack about 7.5 cm/3 inches below the heat. Brush the chicken thighs with oil and season to taste with salt and pepper. Brush the rack with a little oil, add the chicken thighs, skin-side up, and cook for 20–25 minutes, until the chicken is cooked through and the juices run clear when a skewer is inserted into the thickest part of the meat. Remove from the heat and set aside.
2. Meanwhile, bring a large saucepan of lightly salted water to the boil. Add the pasta, return to the boil and cook for 8–10 minutes, or until tender but still firm to the bite. Add the beans 5 minutes before the end of the cooking time.
3. Drain the pasta and beans, shaking off the excess water, and immediately tip into a large bowl. Add the pesto and stir until the pasta and beans are well coated. Set aside to cool.
4. When the chicken is cool enough to handle, remove the skin and bones and cut the flesh into bite-sized pieces. Stir into the pesto mixture and season to taste with salt and pepper. Set aside to cool completely, then cover and chill until required. (It will keep for up to 1 day, covered, in the refrigerator.)

5 Remove the salad from the refrigerator 10 minutes before serving. Arrange the tomato slices on a serving platter. Stir the salad and add extra pesto, if needed. Mound the salad on top of the tomatoes, garnish with basil leaves and serve immediately.

CHICKEN, BACON & AVOCADO SALAD

Serves: 4

Prep: 20 mins, plus cooling

Cook: 20 mins

Ingredients

- 150 g/5½ oz dried farfalle
- 2 thick rashers smoked streaky bacon
- 200 g/7 oz skinless, boneless cooked chicken breasts, sliced
- 2 plum tomatoes, sliced
- 1 large avocado, halved, stoned and sliced
- 35 g/1¼ oz rocket
- salt and pepper

Dressing

- 6 tbsp olive oil
- 3 tbsp lemon juice
- 1 tsp Dijon mustard
- 1–2 garlic cloves, crushed
- salt and pepper

Method

1. Bring a large saucepan of lightly salted water to the boil. Add the pasta, bring back to the boil and cook for 8–10 minutes, until tender but still firm to the bite. Meanwhile place all the ingredients for the dressing in a screw-top jar, and season to taste with salt and pepper. Place the lid on tightly and shake well to combine.
2. Drain the pasta and transfer to a large bowl. Add half the dressing, then toss together and leave to cool. Preheat the grill to high.
3. Grill the bacon for 2–3 minutes, turning until crispy. Transfer the bacon to a chopping board and slice into chunky pieces. Add the pieces to the bowl of pasta with the chicken, tomatoes, avocado and rocket. Pour the remaining dressing over the top and toss well. Serve immediately.

1
2
3

HONEY & CHICKEN PASTA SALAD

Serves: 4

Prep: 15 mins, plus cooling

Cook: 15 mins

Ingredients

- 250 g/9 oz dried fusilli
- 2 tbsp olive oil
- 1 onion, thinly sliced
- 1 garlic clove, crushed
- 400 g/14 oz skinless, boneless chicken breasts, chopped
- 2 tbsp wholegrain mustard
- 2 tbsp clear honey
- 175 g/6 oz cherry tomatoes, halved
- handful of rocket or mizuna leaves
- fresh thyme leaves, to garnish
- salt

Dressing

- 3 tbsp olive oil
- 1 tbsp sherry vinegar
- 2 tsp clear honey
- 1 tbsp fresh thyme leaves
- salt and pepper

Method

1. To make the dressing, place all the ingredients in a small bowl and whisk together.
2. Bring a large saucepan of lightly salted water to the boil. Add the pasta, bring back to the boil and cook for 8–10 minutes, until tender but still firm to the bite.
3. Meanwhile, heat the oil in a large frying pan. Add the onion and garlic and fry for 5 minutes.
4. Add the chicken and cook, stirring frequently, for 3–4 minutes until the chicken is tender and cooked through. Stir the mustard and honey into the pan and cook for a further 2–3 minutes until the chicken and onion are golden brown and sticky.
5. Drain the pasta and transfer to a serving bowl. Pour over the dressing and toss. Stir in the chicken and onion and leave to cool.
6. Gently stir the tomatoes and rocket into the pasta. Serve immediately garnished with the thyme leaves.

3
4

CURRIED CHICKEN SALAD

Serves: 6

Prep: 20 mins, plus chilling

Cook: No cooking

Ingredients

1 large cooked chicken, weighing 1.5 kg/3 lb 5 oz

300 g/10½ oz seedless grapes, halved

2 spring onions, chopped

75 g/2¾ oz celery, diced

35 g/1¼ oz flaked almonds

35 g/1¼ oz red pepper, diced

Dressing

225 ml/8 fl oz mayonnaise

2 tbsp ready-made mango chutney

1 tbsp curry powder

1 tsp ground cumin

juice of 1 lemon

juice of 1 lime

2 tsp soy sauce

Method

1. Carve the chicken carefully, slicing the white meat. Divide the legs into thighs and drumsticks, and trim the wings. Cover with clingfilm and chill in the refrigerator.
2. To make the dressing, combine all the ingredients in a bowl, mix well and reserve.
3. Combine the chicken, grapes, spring onions, celery, almonds and red pepper in a large mixing bowl. Add the dressing and stir to combine. Chill for at least 1 hour before serving.

CHICKEN SALAD CUPS

Makes: 20

Prep: 40 mins, plus cooling

Cook: 10–15 mins

Ingredients

1 loaf thinly sliced white bread

unsalted butter or margarine, softened

225 g/8 oz skinless, boneless cooked chicken, finely chopped

115 g/4 oz celery, finely chopped

35 g/1¼ oz toasted pecans, finely chopped

1 tsp mustard

1 tsp lemon juice

mayonnaise

salt and pepper

Method

1 Preheat the oven to 160°C/325°F/Gas Mark 3. Roll the bread slices flat with a rolling pin. Lightly butter one side of each slice of bread. Cut a round from each slice, using a small cookie or biscuit cutter. Press the rounds into ramekins, buttered side up. Bake in the preheated oven for 10–15 minutes, or until lightly browned. Remove from the ramekins and cool completely.

2 Combine the chicken, celery, pecans, mustard, and lemon juice in a bowl stirring gently. Add enough mayonnaise to moisten the chicken mixture. Season to taste with salt and pepper. Fill the toast cups with the chicken mixture and serve immediately.

CHICKEN WALDORF SALAD

Serves: 6

Prep: 25 mins plus, cooling & chilling

Cook: 20 mins

Ingredients

3 skinless, boneless chicken breasts

1 bay leaf

125 g/4 oz walnuts, halved

90 ml/3 fl oz mayonnaise

2 tbsp freshly squeezed lemon juice

1 tbsp natural yogurt

3 large apples, cored and cut into 2.5-cm/1-inch chunks

150 g/5 oz green or red seedless grapes, halved

75 g/2 oz celery, cut into 5-mm/¼-inch thick slices

1 small butterhead lettuce

salt and pepper

Method

1 Place the chicken breasts, bay leaf and ½ teaspoon of salt in a saucepan. Add just enough water to cover. Heat over a medium–high heat until simmering. Reduce the heat to low, cover and cook for 12 minutes, until the chicken is cooked through and the juices run clear when a skewer is inserted into the thickest part of the meat. Remove the chicken using a slotted spoon, leave to cool, then chill in the refrigerator until required. When ready to serve, cut into 2.5-cm/1-inch cubes.

2 Preheat the oven to 180°C/350°F/Gas Mark 4. Arrange the walnuts on a baking sheet and bake in the preheated oven for 8 minutes. Leave to cool on a chopping board, then roughly chop and reserve.

3 Put the mayonnaise, lemon juice, yogurt, and salt and pepper to taste into a large mixing bowl. Whisk to combine thoroughly. Use a spatula to fold in the apples, grapes, celery, walnuts and chicken, mixing well until evenly coated with the dressing.

4 Arrange a few lettuce leaves on each plate and spoon the salad over the top. Serve immediately.

RED CHICKEN SALAD

Serves: 4

Prep: 20 mins, plus marinating

Cook: 15 mins

Ingredients

- 4 skinless, boneless chicken breasts
- 2 tbsp Thai red curry paste
- 2 tbsp vegetable or peanut oil
- 175 g/6 oz pak choi, torn into large pieces
- ½ savoy cabbage, shredded
- 2 shallots, finely chopped
- 2 garlic cloves, crushed
- 1 tbsp rice wine vinegar
- 2 tbsp sweet chilli sauce
- 2 tbsp Thai soy sauce
- 1 head Chinese leaves, shredded

Method

1. Slash the flesh of the chicken several times and rub the curry paste into each cut. Cover and marinate in the refrigerator overnight.
2. Heat a wok over a high heat, then add 1 tablespoon of the oil. Add the chicken breasts and cook for 5–6 minutes, turning once or twice, until the chicken is cooked through and the juices run clear when a skewer is inserted into the thickest part of the meat. Remove from the wok, set aside and keep warm.
3. Heat the remaining oil in the wok and stir-fry the pak choi and cabbage until just wilted. Add the shallots and garlic, and stir-fry until just tender but not browned. Add the vinegar, chilli sauce and soy sauce. Remove from the heat.
4. Arrange the Chinese leaves on four serving plates. Slice the chicken, arrange on the salad leaves and drizzle the hot dressing over. Serve immediately.

1
3
4

SMOKED CHICKEN & CRANBERRY SALAD

Serves: 4

Prep: 35 mins, plus chilling & soaking

Cook: 2–3 mins

Ingredients

- 1 cooked smoked chicken, weighing 1.3 kg/3 lb
- 115 g/4 oz dried cranberries
- 2 tbsp apple juice or water
- 200 g/7 oz mangetout
- 2 ripe avocados
- juice of ½ lemon
- 4 lettuce hearts
- 1 bunch of watercress
- 55 g/2 oz rocket leaves
- 55 g/2 oz chopped walnuts, (optional)

Dressing

- 2 tbsp olive oil
- 1 tbsp walnut oil
- 2 tbsp lemon juice
- 1 tbsp chopped fresh mixed herbs, such as parsley and lemon thyme
- salt and pepper

Method

1. Carve the chicken carefully, slicing the white meat. Divide the legs into thighs and drumsticks, and trim the wings. Cover with clingfilm and chill in the refrigerator.
2. Put the cranberries in a bowl. Stir in the apple juice, cover with clingfilm and leave to soak for 30 minutes.
3. Meanwhile, bring a large saucepan of water to the boil. Blanch the mangetout for about 30 seconds then refresh under cold running water and drain.
4. Peel, stone and slice the avocados, then toss in the lemon juice to prevent discoloration.
5. Separate the lettuce hearts and arrange on a large serving platter with the avocados, mangetout, watercress, rocket and chicken.
6. To make the dressing, put all the ingredients into a screw-top jar and shake well. Alternatively, put them in a bowl and mix together well.
7. Drain the cranberries and mix them with the dressing, then pour over the salad. Scatter the walnuts, if using, over the salad and serve immediately.

2
3
6

CHICKEN CAESAR SALAD

Serves: 4 **Prep: 25 mins** **Cook: 10 mins**

Ingredients

3 tbsp sunflower oil

2 thick slices of white bread, cubed

3 skinless, boneless chicken breasts

2 small heads of cos lettuce, roughly chopped

2 tbsp Parmesan cheese shavings

salt and pepper

Dressing

1 garlic clove, crushed

2 canned anchovy fillets, drained and finely chopped

5 tbsp light olive oil

2 tbsp white wine vinegar

2 tbsp mayonnaise

2 tbsp freshly grated Parmesan cheese

salt and pepper

Method

1. Preheat the oven to 200°C/400°F/Gas Mark 6. Place 2 tablespoons of the sunflower oil in a bowl, add the bread and toss to coat in the oil. Spread out on a baking sheet, season well with salt and pepper and bake in the preheated oven for 10 minutes, until crisp and golden brown.
2. Meanwhile preheat a griddle pan to medium. Brush the chicken breasts with the remaining sunflower oil and season to taste with salt and pepper. Cook for 8–10 minutes on each side, until the chicken is cooked through and the juices run clear when a skewer is inserted into the thickest part of the meat.
3. To make the dressing, place all the ingredients in a small bowl and mix thoroughly until creamy.
4. Slice the hot cooked chicken and toss lightly with the lettuce and croûtons. Divide the salad between four serving bowls and drizzle over the dressing. Scatter over the Parmesan cheese shavings and serve immediately.

★ Variation

Add spice to the dressing with a teaspoon of paprika or some chopped fresh chillies, then serve in wraps.

QUICK & EASY

OVEN-FRIED CHICKEN WINGS 58

CHICKEN-LOADED POTATO SKINS 60

SPICY CHICKEN PITTAS 62

PIRI PIRI CHICKEN 64

CHICKEN SATAY SKEWERS 66

CHICKEN FRIED RICE 68

GARLIC CHICKEN WITH LEEKS 69

STICKY GINGER & SOY CHICKEN WINGS 70

CHICKEN & LIME TACOS 72

CHICKEN & APPLE BITES 74

CHICKEN THIGHS WITH BARBECUE SAUCE 76

PESTO CHICKEN PIZZA 78

MINCED CHICKEN SKEWERS 79

CHICKEN CHOW MEIN 80

MEDITERRANEAN PAN BAGNA 81

HONEY & MUSTARD CHICKEN 82

FETTUCCINE WITH CHICKEN & BASIL PESTO 84

JERK CHICKEN SKEWERS WITH RICE 86

CREAMY CHICKEN HASH 88

CHICKEN, MUSHROOM & HERB OMELETTE 90

CHICKEN CROSTINI 92

CHICKEN BALLS WITH DIPPING SAUCE 94

QUICK CHICKEN NACHOS 96

CHICKEN WRAPS 97

THAI CHICKEN CAKES 98

CHICKEN FAJITAS 100

CHICKEN WITH MUSTARD CREAM SAUCE 102

SMOKED CHICKEN & HAM FOCACCIA 104

OVEN-FRIED CHICKEN WINGS

Serves: 4 **Prep: 15 mins** **Cook: 20 mins**

Ingredients

12 chicken wings
1 egg
50 ml/2 fl oz milk
4 heaped tbsp plain flour
1 tsp paprika
225 g/8 oz fresh breadcrumbs
55 g/2 oz butter, melted
salt and pepper

Method

1 Preheat the oven to 220°C/425°F/Gas Mark 7. Cut each of the chicken wings into three pieces. Discard the bony tip. Beat the egg with the milk in a shallow dish. Combine the flour, paprika and salt and pepper to taste in a separate shallow dish. Place the breadcrumbs in another shallow dish.

2 Dip the chicken pieces into the seasoned flour and coat first in the egg mixture, allowing any excess to drip back into the dish, then in the breadcrumbs.

3 Pour the melted butter into a shallow roasting tin that is large enough to hold all the chicken pieces in a single layer. Arrange the chicken, skin side down, in the tin and bake in the preheated oven for 10 minutes. Turn and bake for a further 10 minutes, until the chicken is cooked through and the juices run clear when a skewer is inserted into the thickest part of the meat.

4 Remove the chicken from the tin and arrange on a large platter. Serve hot or at room temperature.

★ Variation

Add a teaspoon of cayenne pepper with the paprika for chicken wings with a kick.

CHICKEN-LOADED POTATO SKINS

Serves: 4 **Prep: 20 mins** **Cook: 15 mins**

Ingredients

4 cooked jacket potatoes, halved lengthways

2 tbsp sunflower oil, plus extra for oiling

1 onion, finely chopped

2 tbsp plain flour

freshly grated nutmeg, to taste

300 ml/10 fl oz milk

200 g/7 oz skinless, boneless cooked chicken, diced

200 g/7 oz cooked ham, diced

2 sun-dried tomatoes in oil, drained and thinly sliced

2 tbsp chopped fresh flat-leaf parsley, plus extra to garnish

125 g/4½ oz mozzarella cheese, drained and grated

salt and pepper

Method

1. Preheat the grill to high and position a rack 13 cm/5 inches from the heat.
2. Scoop out the potato flesh, leaving a 5-mm/¼-inch shell. (The flesh can be used in other recipes.) Rub the potato skins with oil, then season with salt and pepper.
3. Place the skins on a baking sheet, cut side up, place under the grill and cook for 5 minutes. Turn and cook for a further 3–5 minutes until crisp. Remove from the heat, but do not switch off the grill.
4. Meanwhile, heat the oil in a saucepan. Add the onion and fry for 2–3 minutes until soft. Add the flour and nutmeg and stir for 2 minutes, then slowly stir in the milk. Bring to the boil, then reduce the heat and simmer for 2 minutes.
5. Stir in the chicken, ham, tomatoes and parsley and season to taste with salt and pepper.
6. Divide the mixture between the potato skins and sprinkle with the cheese. Return to the grill and cook for 4–5 minutes until the filling is piping hot and the cheese is bubbling. Sprinkle with flat-leaf parsley and serve.

SPICY CHICKEN PITTAS

Serves: 4 **Prep: 20 mins** **Cook: 10 mins**

Ingredients

4 pittas, cut in half, to serve

Filling

1 small onion, very thinly sliced

450 g/1 lb skinless, boneless chicken breasts, chopped

½ tsp dried oregano

¼ tsp cayenne pepper

⅛ tsp ground cinnamon

1 tbsp olive oil

salt

Yogurt sauce

1 garlic clove, finely chopped

finely grated zest of 1 lemon

1 tbsp lemon juice

115 ml/4 fl oz natural yogurt

¼ tsp chilli sauce, or to taste

70 g/2½ oz cucumber, grated

¼ tsp chopped fresh flat-leaf parsley

Method

1 Put the sauce ingredients into a small bowl and stir to combine.

2 Add all the filling ingredients to a mixing bowl and mix well.

3 Heat a large frying pan over a high heat until very hot. Add the filling mixture and sauté for 5 minutes, until the chicken is tender and cooked through. Fill the pitta halves with chicken and spoon in the yogurt sauce. Serve immediately.

PIRI PIRI CHICKEN

Serves: 4 **Prep: 10 mins** **Cook: 20–25 mins**

Ingredients

- 8 chicken drumsticks
- 1½ tsp crushed dried red chillies
- 2 garlic cloves, crushed
- 1 tsp dried oregano
- 2 tsp smoked paprika
- juice of ½ lemon
- salt and pepper

To serve

- lemon wedges
- mixed salad leaves
- flatbread

Method

1. Preheat the oven to 220°C/425°F/Gas Mark 7. Cut deep slashes into the thickest parts of the meat.
2. Place the chillies, garlic, oregano, paprika and lemon juice in a large mixing bowl. Season to taste with salt and pepper and mix together. Add the chicken and turn to coat evenly.
3. Arrange the chicken in a single layer in a large, shallow roasting tin. Bake in the preheated oven for 20–25 minutes, turning occasionally, until the chicken is cooked through and the juices run clear when a skewer is inserted into the thickest part of the meat.
4. Transfer to warmed serving plates. Serve immediately with lemon wedges, mixed salad leaves and flatbread.

2
2

CHICKEN SATAY SKEWERS

Serves: 4 **Prep: 15 mins** **Cook: 6–8 mins**

Ingredients

- 4 skinless, boneless chicken breasts, diced
- 4 tbsp soy sauce
- 1 tbsp cornflour
- 2 garlic cloves, finely chopped
- 2.5-cm/1-inch piece fresh ginger, peeled and finely chopped
- 1 cucumber, diced, to serve

Peanut sauce

- 2 tbsp groundnut oil or vegetable oil
- ½ onion, finely chopped
- 1 garlic clove, finely chopped
- 4 tbsp crunchy peanut butter
- 4–5 tbsp water
- ½ tsp chilli powder

Method

1. Put the chicken cubes in a shallow dish. Mix the soy sauce, cornflour, garlic and ginger together in a small bowl and pour over the chicken.
2. Meanwhile, preheat the grill to hot. Thread the chicken onto 12 pre-soaked, wooden skewers. Cook the skewers under the preheated grill for 3–4 minutes or until the chicken is tender and cooked through.
3. Meanwhile, to make the sauce, heat the oil in a saucepan, add the onion and garlic and cook over a medium heat, stirring frequently, for 3–4 minutes until softened. Add the peanut butter, water and chilli powder and simmer for 2–3 minutes until softened and thinned. Serve the skewers immediately with the warm sauce and cucumber.

CHICKEN FRIED RICE

Serves: 4 **Prep: 15 mins** **Cook: 20 mins**

Ingredients

½ tbsp sesame oil
6 shallots, quartered
450 g/1 lb skinless, boneless cooked chicken, diced
3 tbsp soy sauce
2 carrots, diced
1 celery stick, diced
1 red pepper, deseeded and diced
175 g/6 oz peas, thawed if frozen
100 g/3½ oz canned sweetcorn, drained
275 g/9¾ oz cooked long-grain rice
2 large eggs, scrambled

Method

1 Heat the oil in a large frying pan over a medium heat. Add the shallots and cook until soft, then add the chicken and 2 tablespoons of the soy sauce and stir-fry until the chicken is piping hot.

2 Stir in the carrots, celery, red pepper, peas and sweetcorn, and stir-fry for a further 5 minutes. Add the rice and stir thoroughly.

3 Finally, stir in the scrambled eggs and the remaining soy sauce. Serve immediately.

GARLIC CHICKEN WITH LEEKS

Serves: 4 **Prep: 15 mins** **Cook: 10 mins**

Ingredients

450 g/1 lb skinless, boneless chicken breasts, finely chopped

1 tbsp peanut oil

6 garlic cloves, thinly sliced

2.5-cm/1-inch piece finely grated fresh ginger

200 g/7 oz leeks, thinly sliced

4 spring onions, chopped

1 tbsp clear honey

Marinade

2 tbsp rice wine

2 tbsp dark soy sauce

1 tsp sesame oil

Method

1. To make the marinade place the rice wine, soy sauce and sesame oil in a large mixing bowl. Add the chicken and mix together.
2. Drain the chicken, reserving the marinade. Preheat a wok or large frying pan over a high heat. Add the oil and heat until very hot. Add the drained chicken and stir-fry for 3 minutes to seal.
3. Add the garlic, ginger, leeks and spring onions to the wok and fry for a further 3 minutes to soften. Add the reserved marinade and honey and stir-fry for a further minute, until the chicken is tender and cooked through.
4. Transfer to warmed serving bowls and serve immediately.

STICKY GINGER & SOY CHICKEN WINGS

Serves: 4 **Prep: 15 mins** **Cook: 12–15 mins**

Ingredients

- 12 chicken wings
- 2 garlic cloves, crushed
- 2.5-cm/1-inch piece fresh ginger, peeled and chopped
- 2 tbsp dark soy sauce
- 2 tbsp lime juice
- 1 tbsp clear honey
- 1 tsp chilli sauce
- 2 tsp sesame oil
- lime wedges, to serve

Method

1. Tuck the pointed tip of each wing under the thicker end to make a neat triangle.
2. Mix together the garlic, ginger, soy sauce, lime juice, honey, chilli sauce and oil.
3. Spoon the mixture over the chicken and turn to coat evenly.
4. Preheat the grill to hot. Cook the wings on a foil-lined grill pan for 12–15 minutes, basting often with the marinade, until the chicken is cooked through and the juices run clear when a skewer is inserted into the thickest part of the meat. Serve hot, with lime wedges.

3
4

CHICKEN & LIME TACOS

Makes: 12 **Prep: 20 mins** **Cook: 15 mins**

Ingredients

4 skinless, boneless chicken thighs

2 tbsp freshly squeezed lime juice

1 tbsp sunflower oil, plus extra for oiling

1 tsp chilli powder or paprika, or to taste

1 tsp ground cumin

1 tsp ground coriander

salt and pepper

Coriander & lime rice

175 g/6 oz easy-cook long-grain rice

finely grated rind of 1 lime

2 tbsp finely chopped coriander

To serve

12 crisp corn taco shells, warmed according to the packet instructions

shredded cos lettuce

guacamole

tomato salsa

mature Cheddar cheese or Red Leicester cheese, finely grated

Method

1. Put the chicken thighs into a non-metallic dish and rub all over with the lime juice. Mix together the oil, chilli powder, cumin and ground coriander and season to taste with salt and pepper. Rub all over the chicken thighs.
2. Cook the rice according to the packet instructions. Drain well and transfer to a bowl. Stir in the lime rind.
3. Meanwhile heat a ridged, cast-iron griddle pan over a very high heat. Brush the ridges with oil and reduce the heat to medium. Add the chicken thighs and fry for 4 minutes, brushing once with any leftover marinade. Turn and fry for a further 4 minutes, until the chicken is cooked through and the juices run clear when a skewer is inserted into the thickest part of the meat. Slice into strips.
4. Stir the coriander into the rice and adjust the seasoning, if necessary.
5. To assemble, divide the rice between the taco shells, then add the chicken. Top with lettuce, then add any of the suggested serving accompaniments. Serve immediately.

CHICKEN & APPLE BITES

Makes: 20 **Prep: 25 mins** **Cook: 10 mins**

Ingredients

- 1 eating apple, peeled, cored and grated
- 2 skinless, boneless chicken breasts, chopped
- ½ red onion, finely chopped
- 1 tbsp finely chopped fresh parsley
- 50 g/1¾ oz fresh wholemeal breadcrumbs
- 1 tbsp concentrated chicken stock
- wholemeal flour, for coating
- groundnut oil, for shallow-frying

Method

1. Spread the apple out on a clean tea towel and press out all the excess moisture.
2. Put the chicken, apple, onion, parsley, breadcrumbs and stock in a food processor and pulse briefly until well combined.
3. Spread the flour out on a plate. Divide the mixture into 20 portions, shape each portion into a ball and roll in the flour.
4. Heat enough oil for shallow-frying in a non-stick frying pan over a medium heat and cook the balls for 5–8 minutes, or until golden brown all over and cooked through. Remove and drain on kitchen paper. Serve hot or cold.

CHICKEN THIGHS WITH BARBECUE SAUCE

Serves: 4 **Prep: 15 mins** **Cook: 15–20 mins**

Ingredients

- 8 skinless, boneless chicken thighs
- 5 tbsp tomato ketchup
- 2 tbsp soy sauce
- 1 tbsp grated fresh ginger
- 1 garlic clove, crushed
- 1 tbsp olive oil
- salt and pepper

Method

1. Preheat the oven to 220°C/425°F/Gas Mark 7. Cut deep slashes into the thickest parts of the meat.
2. Place the ketchup, soy sauce, ginger, garlic and oil in a large mixing bowl. Season to taste with salt and pepper and mix together. Add the chicken and turn to coat evenly.
3. Arrange the chicken in a single layer in a large, shallow roasting tin. Bake in the preheated oven for 15–20 minutes, turning occasionally, until the chicken is cooked through and the juices run clear when a skewer is inserted into the thickest part of the meat.
4. Transfer to warmed serving plates and serve immediately.

2
2

PESTO CHICKEN PIZZA

Makes: 2 x 26-cm/ 10½-inch pizzas **Prep: 15 mins** **Cook: 10–12 mins**

Ingredients

- 2 x 26-cm/10½-inch ready-made pizza bases
- 8 tbsp ready-made pesto
- 175 g/6 oz skinless, boneless-cooked chicken, torn into strips
- 100 g/3½ oz canned sweetcorn, drained
- 6 cherry tomatoes, thinly sliced
- 250 g/9 oz mozzarella cheese, drained and roughly torn
- salt and pepper

Method

1. Preheat the oven to 220°C/425°F/Gas Mark 7. Place the pizza bases on two baking trays.
2. Divide the pesto between the two pizza bases, spreading almost to the edges. Scatter over the chicken, sweetcorn and tomatoes. Top with the cheese and season to taste with salt and pepper.
3. Bake in the preheated oven for 10–12 minutes, until the chicken is piping hot, the cheese is melted and turning golden and the bases are crisp underneath. Serve immediately.

QUICK & EASY

MINCED CHICKEN SKEWERS

Makes: 8 **Prep: 15 mins** **Cook: 8 mins**

Ingredients

- 450 g/1 lb fresh chicken mince
- 1 onion, finely chopped
- 1 fresh red chilli, deseeded and chopped
- 2 tbsp Thai red curry paste
- 1 tsp palm sugar or soft light brown sugar
- 1 tsp ground coriander
- 1 tsp ground cumin
- 1 egg white
- 8 lemon grass stalks
- cooked rice with chopped spring onion, to serve
- coriander sprigs, to garnish

Method

1. Mix the chicken, onion, chilli, curry paste and sugar together in a bowl to a thick paste. Stir in the coriander, cumin and egg white and mix again.
2. Preheat the grill to high. Divide the mixture into 8 equal portions and squeeze each one around a lemon grass stalk. Arrange on a grill rack and cook under the preheated grill, turning frequently, for 8 minutes, or until browned and cooked through. Serve immediately, accompanied by cooked rice with chopped spring onion stirred through it. Garnish with the coriander sprigs.

CHICKEN CHOW MEIN

Serves: 4 **Prep: 15 mins** **Cook: 15 mins**

Ingredients

- 250 g/9 oz dried medium egg noodles
- 2 tbsp sunflower oil
- 275 g/9¾ oz skinless, boneless cooked chicken breasts, torn into strips
- 1 garlic clove, finely chopped
- 1 red pepper, deseeded and thinly sliced
- 100 g/3½ oz shiitake mushrooms, sliced
- 6 spring onions, sliced
- 100 g/3½ oz fresh beansprouts
- 3 tbsp soy sauce
- 1 tbsp sesame oil

Method

1. Place the noodles in a large bowl or dish and break them up slightly. Pour enough boiling water over the noodles to cover and leave to stand. Alternatively, cook according to the packet instructions.
2. Heat the sunflower oil in a large preheated wok. Add the chicken, garlic, red pepper, mushrooms, spring onions and beansprouts to the wok and stir-fry for about 5 minutes until the chicken is piping hot.
3. Drain the noodles thoroughly. Add the noodles to the wok, toss well and stir-fry for a further 5 minutes.
4. Drizzle the soy sauce and sesame oil over the chow mein and toss until well combined. Transfer to warmed bowls and serve immediately.

MEDITERRANEAN PAN BAGNA

Serves: 2 **Prep: 15 mins** **Cook: No cooking**

Ingredients

- 1 garlic clove, halved
- 1 large baguette, sliced lengthways
- 4 tbsp olive oil
- 140 g/5 oz skinless, boneless cooked chicken, thinly sliced
- 2 large tomatoes, sliced
- 20 g/¾ oz canned anchovy fillets, drained
- 8 large stoned black olives, chopped
- pepper

Method

1. Rub the garlic over the cut side of the baguette and sprinkle with the oil.
2. Arrange the chicken on top of the bread. Place the tomato slices and anchovies on top of the chicken.
3. Scatter with the black olives and season with plenty of pepper. Sandwich the baguette back together and wrap tightly in foil until required. Cut in half to serve.

HONEY & MUSTARD CHICKEN

Serves: 4 **Prep: 10 mins** **Cook: 15–20 mins**

Ingredients

8 chicken pieces
2 tbsp Dijon mustard
2 tbsp Worcestershire sauce
1 tbsp clear honey
salt and pepper
crusty bread, to serve

Method

1. Preheat the oven to 220°C/425°F/Gas Mark 7. Trim any excess fat from the chicken and cut deep slashes into the thickest parts of the meat.
2. Place the mustard, Worcestershire sauce and honey in a large mixing bowl. Season to taste with salt and pepper and mix together. Add the chicken and turn to coat evenly.
3. Arrange the chicken in a single layer in a large, shallow roasting tin. Bake in the preheated oven for 15–20 minutes, turning occasionally, until the chicken is cooked through and the juices run clear when a skewer is inserted into the thickest part of the meat.
4. Transfer to a warmed serving dish and serve immediately with crusty bread.

2
3

FETTUCCINE WITH CHICKEN & BASIL PESTO

Serves: 4 **Prep: 20 mins** **Cook: 10-12 mins**

Ingredients

- 2 tbsp vegetable oil
- 4 skinless, boneless chicken breasts
- 350 g/12 oz dried fettuccine
- salt and pepper

Pesto

- 100 g/3½ oz shredded fresh basil, plus extra sprigs to garnish
- 125 ml/4 fl oz extra virgin olive oil
- 3 tbsp pine kernels
- 3 garlic cloves, crushed
- generous pinch of salt
- 55 g/2 oz freshly grated Parmesan cheese
- 2 tbsp freshly grated pecorino cheese

Method

1. To make the pesto, put the shredded basil, olive oil, pine kernels, garlic and a salt in a food processor or blender. Process the ingredients until smooth. Scrape the mixture into a bowl and stir in the cheeses.
2. Heat the vegetable oil in a frying pan over a medium heat. Cook the chicken breasts, turning once, for 8–10 minutes, until the chicken is cooked through and the juices run clear when a skewer is inserted into the thickest part of the meat. Cut into small cubes.
3. Meanwhile, bring a large saucepan of lightly salted water to the boil. Add the pasta, bring back to the boil and cook for 8–10 minutes, or until tender but still firm to the bite.
4. Drain the pasta and return to the pan. Add the chicken and pesto, then season to taste with pepper. Toss well to mix. Transfer to serving dishes, garnish with basil sprigs and serve immediately.

JERK CHICKEN SKEWERS WITH RICE

Serves: 4

Prep: 15 mins, plus standing

Cook: 15 mins

Ingredients

500 g/1 lb 2 oz skinless, boneless chicken thighs, chopped

200 g/7 oz basmati rice

1 tbsp finely grated lime rind

2 tbsp coriander

salt

lime wedges, to serve

Jerk sauce

1 small onion, quartered

1 garlic clove

2 green finger chillies

2.5-cm/1-inch piece fresh ginger

1 tsp ground allspice

1½ tsp dried thyme

juice of ½ lime

2 tbsp olive oil

Method

1 To make the sauce, place all the ingredients in a food processor or blender and process until smooth. Tip into a bowl and stir in the chunks of chicken. Cover and leave to stand for 5 minutes.

2 Cook the rice in a saucepan of lightly salted water for 10–12 minutes, until tender. Drain. Stir in the lime rind and coriander, cover the pan with a clean tea towel and leave to stand.

3 Meanwhile, preheat the grill to hot. Thread the chicken onto eight pre-soaked, wooden skewers. Cook the skewers under the preheated grill for 12–15 minutes, turning occasionally, until the chicken is tender and cooked through.

4 Transfer to warmed serving plates. Serve immediately with the lime and coriander rice and lime wedges.

1
2

CREAMY CHICKEN HASH

Serves: 4–6 **Prep: 10 mins** **Cook: 25 mins**

Ingredients

- 3 tbsp sunflower oil
- 450 g/1 lb fresh chicken mince
- 1 tsp dried thyme or dried dill
- pinch of cayenne pepper
- 1 onion, finely chopped
- 1 large red pepper, deseeded and finely chopped
- 2 large garlic cloves, finely chopped
- 2 tbsp plain flour
- 300 ml/10 fl oz milk
- 100 g/3½ oz frozen peas
- 200 g/7 oz canned sweetcorn kernels, drained and rinsed
- salt and pepper

Method

1. Heat 2 tablespoons of the oil in a large frying pan over a medium–high heat. Add the chicken, thyme, cayenne pepper, and salt and pepper to taste and fry, stirring with a wooden spoon to break up the chicken into large clumps, for 4–6 minutes until just starting to brown. Transfer to a bowl using a slotted spoon and set aside.
2. Add the remaining oil to the pan, then add the onion and red pepper and fry, stirring, for 3–5 minutes until the onion is soft. Add the garlic and stir for a further 30 seconds.
3. Sprinkle over the flour and stir for about 1 minute. Slowly stir in the milk and continue stirring until a smooth, creamy sauce forms.
4. Return the chicken to the pan and add the peas and sweetcorn. Bring to the boil, stirring, then reduce the heat and simmer, uncovered, for 5 minutes, or until the peas are tender and the chicken is cooked through. Adjust the salt and pepper, if necessary. Serve immediately.

CHICKEN, MUSHROOM & HERB OMELETTE

Makes: 1 **Prep: 15 mins** **Cook: 12–15 mins**

Ingredients

15 g/½ oz butter

2 tbsp sunflower oil

100 g/3½ oz chestnut mushrooms, trimmed and thinly sliced

55 g/2 oz skinless, boneless cooked chicken, chopped

1 tbsp chopped mixed fresh herbs, such as chervil, chives, parsley and thyme, plus extra parsley to garnish

2 eggs

1 tbsp milk or water

salt and pepper

Method

1. Melt the butter with half the oil in a 20-cm/8-inch frying pan over a medium–high heat. Add the mushrooms, season to taste with salt and pepper and fry, stirring, for 5–8 minutes until the mushrooms re-absorb the liquid they give off.
2. Add the chicken and herbs and continue frying to heat the chicken until piping hot. Adjust the seasoning, if necessary. Remove from the pan and keep hot.
3. Add the remaining oil to the pan, heat until hot and swirl around the base and side. Beat the eggs with the milk and season to taste with salt and pepper.
4. When the oil is hot, pour the eggs into the pan, tilting and rotating the pan so they cover the base evenly. Reduce the heat to low–medium.
5. Cook for 5–10 seconds, or until the omelette is set on the base. Spoon the chicken mixture into the centre, then use a palette knife to ease half the omelette over the filling. Slide the omelette out of the pan, garnish with parsley and serve immediately.

3
4

CHICKEN CROSTINI

Serves: 4 **Prep: 15 mins** **Cook: 10 mins**

Ingredients

12 slices of French bread or rustic bread

4 tbsp olive oil

2 garlic cloves, chopped

2 tbsp fresh oregano, finely chopped, plus extra to garnish

100 g/3½ oz skinless, boneless cooked chicken, cut into thin slices

4 tomatoes, sliced

12 thin slices of goat's cheese

12 black olives, stoned and chopped

salt and pepper

Method

1 Preheat the oven to 180°C/350°F/Gas Mark 4 and the grill to medium. Put the bread under the preheated grill and lightly toast on both sides.

2 Meanwhile, pour the oil into a bowl and add the garlic and oregano. Season to taste with salt and pepper and mix well. Remove the toasted bread slices from the grill and spoon a little of the oil mixture on one side only.

3 Place the bread slices, oiled sides up, on a baking sheet. Put some of the sliced chicken on top of each one, followed by a slice of tomato. Divide the slices of goat's cheese among them, then top with the olives.

4 Drizzle over the remaining oil mixture and transfer to the preheated oven. Bake for about 5 minutes, or until the cheese is golden and starting to melt. Garnish with oregano and serve immediately.

2
3

CHICKEN BALLS WITH DIPPING SAUCE

Serves: 4 **Prep: 15 mins** **Cook: 15–20 mins**

Ingredients

3 tbsp vegetable oil

2 skinless, boneless chicken breasts, chopped

2 shallots, finely chopped

½ celery stick, finely chopped

1 garlic clove, crushed

2 tbsp light soy sauce

1 small egg, lightly beaten

1 bunch of spring onions

salt and pepper

Dipping sauce

3 tbsp dark soy sauce

1 tbsp rice wine

1 tsp sesame seeds

Method

1 Heat half of the oil in a frying pan and stir-fry the chicken over a high heat for 4–5 minutes, until tender and cooked through. Remove from the pan with a slotted spoon and set aside.

2 Add the shallots, celery and garlic to the pan and stir-fry for 1–2 minutes, until softened.

3 Place the chicken and the shallot mixture in a food processor and process until finely minced. Add 1 tablespoon of the light soy sauce and just enough of the egg to make a fairly firm mixture. Season to taste with salt and pepper.

4 To make the dipping sauce, mix together the dark soy sauce, rice wine and sesame seeds in a small serving bowl and set aside.

5 Shape the chicken mixture into 16 walnut-sized balls. Heat the remaining oil in the pan and stir-fry the chicken balls in small batches for 4–5 minutes, until golden brown and cooked through. Drain on kitchen paper.

6 Add the spring onions to the pan and stir-fry for 1–2 minutes, until they begin to soften, then stir in the remaining light soy sauce. Serve the chicken balls with the stir-fried spring onions and the dipping sauce.

QUICK CHICKEN NACHOS

Serves: 4 **Prep: 15 mins** **Cook: 10–15 mins**

Ingredients

- 100 g/3½ oz salted tortilla chips
- 150 g/5½ oz skinless, boneless cooked chicken, shredded
- 85 g/3 oz Cheddar cheese, grated
- pepper
- 6 tbsp tomato salsa, to serve
- 6 tbsp soured cream, to serve

Method

1. Place a large piece of double-thickness aluminium foil in the base of a non-stick frying pan and place the pan over a medium–high heat.
2. Place the tortilla chips in a single layer on the foil. Scatter over the chicken and cheese. Cover the pan either with a lid or with some foil.
3. Cook the nachos for about 10–15 minutes, until the chicken is piping hot and the cheese is just melted (check by opening up the foil regularly).
4. Season to taste with pepper and serve the nachos with the salsa and soured cream liberally spooned over.

CHICKEN WRAPS

Serves: 4 **Prep: 20 mins** **Cook: No cooking**

Ingredients

- 150 g/5½ oz natural yogurt
- 1 tbsp wholegrain mustard
- 280 g/10 oz skinless, boneless cooked chicken breasts, diced
- 140 g/5 oz Iceberg lettuce, finely shredded
- 85 g/3 oz cucumber, thinly sliced
- 2 celery sticks, sliced
- 85 g/3 oz black seedless grapes, halved
- 4 large flour tortillas
- pepper

Method

1. Combine the yogurt and mustard in a bowl and season to taste with pepper. Stir in the chicken and toss until thoroughly coated.
2. Put the lettuce, cucumber, celery and grapes into a separate bowl and mix well.
3. Fold a tortilla in half and in half again to make a cone that is easy to hold. Half-fill the tortilla pocket with quarter of the salad mixture and top with quarter of the chicken mixture. Repeat with the remaining tortillas, salad and chicken. Serve immediately.

THAI CHICKEN CAKES

Serves: 4 **Prep: 10 mins** **Cook: 25 mins**

Ingredients

- ½ bunch spring onions, trimmed and roughly chopped
- 3-cm/1¼-inch piece fresh ginger, roughly chopped
- 3 garlic cloves, crushed
- handful fresh coriander, including the stalks
- 1 red chilli, deseeded and roughly chopped
- 500 g/1 lb 2 oz fresh chicken mince
- 2 tbsp light soy sauce
- dash of nam pla (Thai fish sauce)
- 1 egg white
- 2 tbsp plain flour
- finely grated zest of 1 lime
- 2–3 tbsp vegetable oil, for frying
- pepper
- lime wedges and sweet chilli sauce, to serve

Method

1. Place the spring onions, ginger, garlic, coriander and chilli in a food processor or blender and process until everything is finely chopped.
2. Tip into a mixing bowl, add the chicken and combine together with the soy sauce, nam pla, egg white, flour, lime zest and pepper to taste.
3. Heat a little oil in a non-stick frying pan and add spoonfuls of the mixture in batches. Cook each batch for about 4 minutes on each side, until golden and cooked through. Transfer to a plate and keep warm while cooking the remaining mixture.
4. Serve the cooked Thai chicken cakes with lime wedges and sweet chilli sauce for dipping.

CHICKEN FAJITAS

Serves: 4 **Prep: 20 mins** **Cook: 12-15 mins**

Ingredients

3 tbsp olive oil, plus extra for drizzling

3 tbsp maple syrup or clear honey

1 tbsp red wine vinegar

2 garlic cloves, crushed

2 tsp dried oregano

1–2 tsp dried chilli flakes

4 skinless, boneless chicken breasts, chopped

2 red peppers, deseeded and cut into 2.5-cm/1-inch strips

salt and pepper

warmed flour tortillas and shredded lettuce, to serve

Method

1. Place the oil, maple syrup, vinegar, garlic, oregano, chilli flakes, and salt and pepper to taste in a large, shallow dish and mix together. Toss the chicken in the marinade to coat.
2. Drain the chicken. Heat a griddle pan until hot. Add the chicken and cook over a medium–high heat for 3–4 minutes on each side until tender and cooked through. Transfer to a warmed plate.
3. Add the peppers, skin side down, to the pan and cook for 2 minutes on each side. Transfer to the plate with the chicken.
4. Divide the chicken and peppers between the flour tortillas, top with a little shredded lettuce, wrap and serve immediately.

2
3

CHICKEN WITH MUSTARD CREAM SAUCE

Serves: 4 **Prep: 10 mins** **Cook: 15 mins**

Ingredients

4 skinless, boneless chicken breasts
1 tbsp butter
125 ml/4 fl oz chicken stock
150 ml/5 fl oz double cream
2 tablespoons stone-ground style mustard
2 tbsp chopped Italian parsley
salt and pepper

Method

1 Place each chicken breast between two sheets of clingfilm and beat firmly with a meat mallet or rolling pin to flatten the chicken to about 1-cm/½ inch thick. Season with salt and pepper.

2 Heat the butter in a large frying pan over medium–high heat. Cook the chicken for about 5 minutes on each side until the chicken is cooked through and the juices run clear when a skewer is inserted into the thickest part of the meat. Transfer to a plate.

3 Add the chicken stock to the pan. Whisk in the cream, mustard, and parsley. Cook for about 3 minutes, until the sauce has thickened. Pour the sauce over the chicken and serve.

SMOKED CHICKEN & HAM FOCACCIA

Serves: 2–4 **Prep: 20 mins** **Cook: 10 mins**

Ingredients

1 thick focaccia loaf
handful of fresh basil leaves
2 small courgettes, coarsely grated
6 wafer-thin slices of smoked chicken
6 wafer-thin slices of cooked ham
225 g/8 oz taleggio cheese, cut into strips
freshly grated nutmeg (optional)
cherry tomatoes and salad leaves, to serve

Method

1 Preheat a griddle plate or pan under the grill until both grill and griddle are hot. If you do not have a griddle, heat a heavy baking sheet instead. Slice the focaccia in half horizontally and cut the top half lengthways into strips.

2 Cover the bottom half of the focaccia with basil leaves, top with the courgettes in an even layer and cover with the chicken and ham. Lay the strips of focaccia on top, placing strips of cheese between them. Sprinkle with a little nutmeg, if using.

3 Place the assembled bread on the hot griddle and cook under the preheated grill, well away from the heat, for about 5 minutes, until the cheese has melted and the top of the bread is browned. Cut the focaccia into four pieces and serve immediately with cherry tomatoes and salad leaves.

★ Variation

Replace the taleggio cheese with blue cheese.

FAMILY MEALS

CHICKEN BREASTS BRAISED WITH BABY VEGETABLES 108
ROAST CHICKEN 110
CREAMY CHICKEN WITH APPLES 112
INDIVIDUAL CHICKEN PIES 114
BACON-WRAPPED CHICKEN BURGERS 116
CHICKEN ESCALOPES WITH GOAT'S CHEESE SAUCE 118
CHICKEN QUESADILLAS 119
STICKY LIME CHICKEN 120
DEEP-PAN CHICKEN FEAST PIZZA 122
CHICKEN WITH TOMATO SAUCE & MELTED MOZZARELLA 124
RISOTTO WITH LEMON CHICKEN 126
THE ULTIMATE CHICKEN BURGER 128
CRISPY CHICKEN FINGERS 129
CHICKEN MEATBALL PASTA 130
CHICKEN KIEV 131
CANNELLONI WITH CHICKEN & HAM 132
CHICKEN FETTUCCINI ALFREDO 134
CHICKEN NOODLE CASSEROLE 136
JERK CHICKEN BURGERS 138
CHICKEN LASANGE 140
CHICKEN & SPICY TOMATO SAUCE PARCELS 142
CHEDDAR & APPLE-STUFFED CHICKEN BREASTS 144
SOUTHERN-STYLE CHICKEN DRUMSTICKS 146
WHITE CHILLI 147
CHICKEN, MUSHROOM & TARRAGON PIE 148
CHICKEN RIGATONI BOLOGNESE 150
FRIED CHICKEN WITH TOMATO & BACON SAUCE 152
CHICKEN CARBONARA 154

CHICKEN BREASTS BRAISED WITH BABY VEGETABLES

Serves: 4 **Prep: 15 mins** **Cook: 30–35 mins**

Ingredients

4 skinless, boneless chicken breasts
15 g/½ oz butter
1 tbsp olive oil
8 shallots
250 ml/9 fl oz chicken stock
12 baby carrots
8 baby turnips
2 bay leaves
140 g/5 oz fresh or frozen peas
salt and pepper
boiled new potatoes, to serve

Method

1 Cut deep slashes through the chicken at intervals and sprinkle with salt and pepper.

2 Heat the butter and oil in a wide, flameproof casserole or saucepan, add the chicken breasts and shallots and fry, turning, for 3–4 minutes until golden brown.

3 Add the stock and bring to the boil, then add the carrots, turnips and bay leaves. Reduce the heat, cover and simmer gently for 20 minutes.

4 Stir in the peas and cook for a further 5 minutes. Check the chicken and vegetables are tender and the juices of the meat run clear when a skewer is inserted into the thickest part of the meat.

5 Remove and discard the bay leaves, adjust the seasoning to taste and serve with new potatoes.

★ Variation

Vary the vegetables you use for a different version of this meal. Try sweet potato chunks, sweetcorn, leeks, beans or whatever you have to hand.

ROAST CHICKEN

Serves: 6

Prep: 20 mins

Cook: 2 hours 5 mins, plus resting

Ingredients

1 whole chicken, weighing 2.25 kg/5 lb

55 g/2 oz butter, softened

2 tbsp chopped fresh lemon thyme, plus extra sprigs to garnish

1 lemon, cut into quarters

125 ml/4 fl oz white wine, plus extra if needed

salt and pepper

Method

1. Preheat the oven to 220°C/425°F/Gas Mark 7. Place the chicken in a roasting tin. Put the butter in a bowl, then mix in the thyme, and salt and pepper to taste and use to butter the chicken.
2. Place the lemon inside the cavity. Pour the wine over and roast in the preheated oven for 15 minutes.
3. Reduce the temperature to 190°C/375°F/Gas Mark 5 and roast, basting frequently, for a further 1¾ hours until the chicken is cooked through and the juices run clear when a skewer is inserted into the thickest part of the meat. Transfer the chicken to a warmed platter, cover with foil and allow to rest for 10 minutes.
4. Place the roasting tin on the hob and simmer the pan juices gently over a low heat until they have reduced and are thick and glossy. Season with salt and pepper.
5. Serve with the pan juices, garnished with thyme sprigs.

2
3

CREAMY CHICKEN WITH APPLES

Serves: 4 **Prep: 15 mins** **Cook: 50 mins–1 hour**

Ingredients

2 tbsp plain flour
4 chicken legs
1 tbsp olive oil
25 g/1 oz butter
1 large leek, sliced
150 ml/5 fl oz chicken stock
150 ml/5 fl oz apple juice
2 tsp wholegrain mustard
5 tbsp crème fraîche
2 red eating apples, cored and thickly sliced
salt and pepper
chopped fresh parsley, to garnish
mashed potatoes, to serve

Method

1. Spread out the flour on a plate and season well with salt and pepper. Toss the chicken legs in the seasoned flour, shaking off any excess. Heat the oil and half the butter in a large frying pan. Fry the chicken legs over a high heat, turning occasionally, for 10 minutes, until golden brown all over.
2. Add the leek and fry for 1 minute. Pour in the stock and apple juice, then cover and simmer for 25–30 minutes, until the chicken is cooked through and the juices run clear when a skewer is inserted into the thickest part of the meat.
3. Using a slotted spoon, remove the chicken from the pan, cover and keep warm. Bring the liquid in the pan to the boil and boil rapidly until reduced by one third. Stir in the mustard and crème fraîche and simmer for 5 minutes, until the sauce has thickened.
4. Heat the remaining butter in a small frying pan and fry the apple slices for 2–3 minutes, until tender and golden. Transfer the chicken and fried apples to plates, pour over the sauce and garnish with parsley. Serve immediately with mashed potatoes.

2
4

INDIVIDUAL CHICKEN PIES

Serves: 6

Prep: 25 mins

Cook: 1 hour 5 mins–1 hour 10 mins,
plus standing

Ingredients

- 1 tbsp olive oil
- 225 g/8 oz button mushrooms, sliced
- 1 onion, finely chopped
- 350 g/12 oz carrots, sliced
- 2 celery sticks, sliced
- 1 litre/1¾ pints cold chicken stock
- 85 g/3 oz butter
- 55 g/2 oz plain flour, plus extra for dusting
- 900 g/2 lb skinless, boneless chicken breasts, diced
- 115 g/4 oz frozen peas
- 1 tsp chopped fresh thyme
- 675 g/1 lb 8 oz ready-made shortcrust pastry
- 1 egg, lightly beaten
- salt and pepper

Method

1. Preheat the oven to 200°C/400°F/Gas Mark 6. Heat the oil in a large saucepan. Add the mushrooms and onion and cook over a medium heat, stirring frequently, for 8 minutes until golden.
2. Add the carrots, celery and half the stock and bring to the boil. Reduce the heat to low and simmer for 12–15 minutes until the vegetables are almost tender.
3. Meanwhile, melt the butter in a large saucepan over a medium heat. Whisk in the flour and cook, stirring constantly, for 4 minutes.
4. Gradually whisk in the remaining stock, then reduce the heat to medium–low and simmer, stirring, until thick. Stir in the vegetable mixture and add the chicken, peas and thyme.
5. Simmer, stirring constantly, for 5 minutes. Taste and adjust the seasoning, adding salt and pepper if needed. Divide the mixture between six large ramekins.
6. Roll out the pastry on a floured surface and cut out six rounds, each 2.5 cm/1 inch larger than the diameter of the ramekins.
7. Place the pastry rounds on top of the filling, then crimp the edges. Cut a small cross in the centre of each round.

8 Put the ramekins on a baking sheet and brush the tops with beaten egg. Bake in the preheated oven for 35–40 minutes, until golden brown and bubbling and the chicken is cooked through. Leave to stand for 15 minutes before serving.

BACON-WRAPPED CHICKEN BURGERS

Serves: 4

Prep: 25 mins, plus chilling

Cook: 15 mins

Ingredients

450 g/1 lb fresh chicken mince
1 onion, grated
2 garlic cloves, crushed
55 g/2 oz pine kernels, toasted
55 g/2 oz Gruyère cheese, grated
2 tbsp snipped fresh chives
2 tbsp wholemeal plain flour
8 slices of lean back bacon
1–2 tbsp sunflower oil
salt and pepper

To serve

4 crusty rolls, split
sliced red onion
lettuce leaves
mayonnaise
chopped spring onions

Method

1. Place the chicken, onion, garlic, pine kernels, cheese, chives and salt and pepper to taste in a food processor. Using the pulse button, blend the mixture together working in short sharp bursts. Scrape out onto a board and shape into four equal-sized burgers. Coat in the flour, then cover and chill in the refrigerator for 1 hour.
2. Wrap each burger in two bacon slices, securing in place with a wooden cocktail stick.
3. Heat a heavy-based frying pan and add the oil. When hot, add the burgers and cook over a medium heat for 5–6 minutes on each side, or until the chicken is golden and cooked through. Remove and discard the cocktail sticks.
4. Serve the burgers in the rolls with sliced red onion, lettuce leaves, a spoonful of mayonnaise and chopped spring onions.

CHICKEN ESCALOPES WITH GOAT'S CHEESE SAUCE

Serves: 4 **Prep: 15 mins** **Cook: 20–25 mins**

Ingredients

- 4 skinless, boneless chicken breasts
- 2 tbsp olive oil
- 115 g/4 oz mushrooms, sliced
- 1 tbsp butter
- 4 tbsp chicken stock
- 125 ml/4 fl oz double cream
- 85 g/3 oz goat's cheese
- 15 g/½ oz chopped fresh parsley
- salt and pepper

Method

1. Halve each chicken breast. Place each half between two sheets of clingfilm and beat firmly with a meat mallet or rolling pin to flatten the chicken to about 5-mm/¼-inch thick escalopes. Season with salt and pepper.
2. Heat the oil in a large frying pan over a medium–high heat. Cook the chicken for about 3 minutes on each side, until the chicken is cooked through and the juices run clear when a skewer is inserted into the thickest part of the meat. Transfer to a plate.
3. Add the mushrooms and butter to the pan and cook, stirring occasionally, until the liquid has evaporated and the mushrooms have browned. Stir in the stock, cream, cheese and parsley. Heat until simmering, then add the chicken and cook until heated through. Season with salt and pepper to taste and serve immediately.

CHICKEN QUESADILLAS

Serves: 4 **Prep: 25 mins** **Cook: 40–45 mins**

Ingredients

3–4 tbsp sunflower oil

1 red onion, thinly sliced

400 g/14 oz skinless, boneless chicken breasts, finely chopped

1 yellow pepper, deseeded and thinly sliced

1 tsp chilli powder

8 flour tortillas

8 tbsp mild salsa

225 g/8 oz Cheddar cheese, grated

4 tbsp chopped fresh coriander

salt and pepper

soured cream, guacamole and lime wedges to serve

Method

1 Heat 1 tablespoon of the oil in a frying pan and fry the onion for 5 minutes, until softened. Add the chicken and yellow pepper and cook over a medium–high heat, stirring frequently, for 10–12 minutes, until the chicken is tender and cooked through. Stir in the chilli powder and season to taste with salt and pepper.

2 Take one of the tortillas and spread with 2 tablespoons of the salsa, leaving a 1-cm/½-inch border around the edge of the tortilla. Spread over a quarter of the chicken mixture and scatter over a quarter of the grated cheese and coriander. Place a second tortilla on top, pressing down gently. Repeat with the remaining ingredients to make four quesadillas in total.

3 Heat a little of the remaining oil in a large frying pan and fry the quesadillas, one at a time, for 3–4 minutes on each side, until crisp and lightly browned, adding more oil as necessary. Cut the quesadillas into quarters and serve immediately with soured cream, guacamole and lime wedges.

STICKY LIME CHICKEN

Serves: 4 **Prep: 15 mins** **Cook: 35–40 mins**

Ingredients

- 4 skinless, part-boned, chicken breasts
- juice and grated rind of 1 lime
- 1 tbsp clear honey
- 1 tbsp olive oil
- 1 garlic clove, chopped (optional)
- 1 tbsp chopped fresh thyme
- pepper
- roasted cherry tomatoes and chargrilled courgettes, to serve
- grated lemon rind, to garnish

Method

1. Preheat the oven to 190°C/375°F/Gas Mark 5. Arrange the chicken breasts in a shallow roasting tin.
2. Put the lime juice and rind, honey, oil, garlic, if using, and thyme in a small bowl and combine thoroughly. Spoon the mixture evenly over the chicken breasts and season to taste with pepper.
3. Roast the chicken in the preheated oven, basting occasionally, for 35–40 minutes, until the chicken is cooked through and the juices run clear when a skewer is inserted into the thickest part of the meat. As the chicken cooks, the liquid in the pan will thicken to give a sticky coating.
4. Remove from the oven and transfer to plates. Garnish with lemon rind and serve immediately with roasted cherry tomatoes and chargrilled courgettes.

2
3

DEEP-PAN CHICKEN FEAST PIZZA

Serves: 2–4

Prep: 20 mins, plus cooling

Cook: 35–40 mins

Ingredients

- 4 tbsp olive oil, plus extra for brushing
- 55 g/2 oz smoked bacon, diced
- 1 onion, finely chopped
- 280 g/10 oz skinless, boneless chicken breasts, diced
- 1 tsp chopped fresh tarragon
- 115 g/4 oz sliced smoked chicken, cut into strips
- 1 x 38-cm/15-inch ready-made pizza base
- pinch of dried oregano
- 140 g/5 oz mozzarella cheese, grated

Method

1. Heat 2 tablespoons of the oil in a frying pan. Add the bacon and onion, and cook over a low heat, stirring occasionally, for 5 minutes, until softened. Add the fresh chicken, increase the heat to medium and stir-fry for 4–5 minutes, until tender and cooked through.
2. Remove the pan from the heat and drain off as much oil as possible. Stir in the tarragon and leave to cool completely. Stir in the smoked chicken.
3. Preheat the oven to 220°C/425°F/Gas Mark 7. Brush a baking sheet or a deep pizza pan with oil.
4. Place the pizza base on the prepared baking sheet and brush with 1 tablespoon of the remaining oil. Spoon the chicken mixture on top and sprinkle with the oregano. Drizzle with the remaining oil and sprinkle with the mozzarella. Bake in the preheated oven for 25–30 minutes, until the cheese is golden and bubbling, and the chicken is piping hot. Serve immediately.

CHICKEN WITH TOMATO SAUCE & MELTED MOZZARELLA

Serves: 6 **Prep: 15 mins** **Cook: 30–35 mins**

Ingredients

6 rashers bacon

25 g/1 oz butter

2 tsp chopped fresh tarragon

6 skinless, boneless chicken breasts

115 g/4 oz mozzarella cheese, sliced

Tomato sauce

25 g/1 oz butter

2 tbsp olive oil

1 onion, finely chopped

2 garlic cloves, finely chopped

1 celery stick, finely chopped

400 g/14 oz canned chopped tomatoes

2 tbsp tomato purée

brown sugar, to taste

1 tsp dried oregano

100 ml/3½ fl oz water

salt and pepper

Method

1 First, make the sauce. Melt the butter with the oil in a saucepan. Add the onion, garlic and celery and cook over a low heat, stirring occasionally, for 5 minutes, until softened. Stir in the tomatoes, tomato purée, sugar to taste, oregano and water and season to taste with salt and pepper. Increase the heat to medium and bring to the boil, then reduce the heat and simmer, stirring occasionally, for 15–20 minutes, until thickened.

2 Meanwhile, fry the bacon without any additional fat in a large frying pan over a medium heat for 5 minutes. Remove with tongs and drain on kitchen paper. Add the butter to the pan and, when it has melted, stir in the tarragon, add the chicken and cook, turning occasionally, for 15–20 minutes, until the chicken is cooked through and the juices run clear when a skewer is inserted into the thickest part of the meat.

3 Preheat the grill. Transfer the chicken to an ovenproof dish and put a bacon rasher on top of each fillet. Pour the sauce over them, cover with the mozzarella slices and cook under the preheated grill for 4–5 minutes, until the cheese has melted and is lightly browned. Serve immediately.

RISOTTO WITH LEMON CHICKEN

Serves: 4

Prep: 20 mins, plus chilling & standing

Cook: 30–35 mins, plus resting

Ingredients

- 4 boneless chicken breasts
- grated rind and juice of 1 lemon
- 5 tbsp olive oil
- 1 garlic clove, crushed
- 8 fresh thyme sprigs, finely chopped, plus extra to garnish
- 1 litre/1¾ pints chicken stock
- 40 g/1½ oz butter
- 1 small onion, finely chopped
- 280 g/10 oz risotto rice
- 150 ml/5 fl oz dry white wine
- 85 g/3 oz freshly grated Parmesan cheese
- salt and pepper
- lemon wedges, to garnish

Method

1. Place the chicken in a shallow, non-metallic dish and season well with salt and pepper. Mix the lemon rind and juice, 4 tablespoons of the oil, the garlic and thyme together and pour over the chicken. Cover and chill for 4–6 hours.
2. Return the chicken to room temperature. Preheat a griddle over a high heat. Put the chicken, skin-side down, on the griddle and cook for 10 minutes. Turn over, reduce the heat and cook for a further 10–15 minutes, until the chicken is cooked through and the juices run clear when a skewer is inserted into the thickest part of the meat. Leave to rest for 5 minutes, then cut into thick slices and keep warm.
3. Meanwhile, bring the stock to the boil in a saucepan, then reduce the heat and keep simmering gently over a low heat while you are cooking the risotto.
4. Heat the remaining oil with 25 g/1 oz of the butter in a deep saucepan over a medium heat. Add the onion and cook, stirring occasionally, for 5 minutes, or until softened. Add the rice and mix to coat in oil and butter. Cook, stirring constantly, for 2–3 minutes, or until the grains are translucent. Add the wine and cook, stirring constantly, until reduced.

5 Gradually add the hot stock, a ladleful at a time. Stir constantly and add more liquid as the rice absorbs each addition. Cook for 20 minutes, or until all the liquid is absorbed and the rice is creamy but still firm to the bite.

6 Remove from the heat and add the remaining butter. Mix well, then stir in the Parmesan until it melts. Season to taste with salt and pepper. Spoon onto warmed plates and top with the chicken. Garnish with lemon wedges and thyme.

THE ULTIMATE CHICKEN BURGER

Serves: 4

Prep: 15 mins, plus chilling

Cook: 15–18 mins

Ingredients

4 large skinless, boneless chicken breasts

1 large egg white

1 tbsp cornflour

1 tbsp plain flour

1 egg, beaten

55 g/2 oz fresh breadcrumbs

2 tbsp sunflower oil

To serve

4 burger buns, split

sliced tomatoes

lettuce leaves

mayonnaise

Method

1 Place each chicken breast between two sheets of clingfilm and beat firmly with a meat mallet or rolling pin to flatten the chicken slightly. Beat together the egg white and cornflour, then brush over the chicken. Cover and leave to chill for 30 minutes, then coat in the plain flour.

2 Place the egg in a shallow dish and the breadcrumbs in a separate shallow dish. Dip the chicken breasts first in the egg, allowing any excess to drip back into the dish, then in the breadcrumbs to coat.

3 Heat a heavy-based frying pan and add the oil. When hot, add the burgers and cook over a medium heat for 6–8 minutes on each side, or until the chicken is tender and the juices run clear when a skewer is inserted into the thickest part of the meat.

4 Serve the burgers in the burger buns with tomato slices, lettuce leaves and a spoonful of mayonnaise.

CRISPY CHICKEN FINGERS

Serves: 8 **Prep: 25 mins, plus standing** **Cook: 30–35 mins**

Ingredients

- 140 g/5 oz plain flour
- 2 tsp salt
- 1 tsp garlic salt
- 1 tsp chipotle chilli powder
- ½ tsp white pepper
- 4 skinless, boneless chicken breasts, cut into thin strips
- 4 eggs, beaten
- 1 tbsp milk
- 175 g/6 oz fine white breadcrumbs
- rapeseed oil, for frying

Method

1. Put the flour, salt, garlic salt, chilli powder and pepper into a large, resealable polythene bag. Shake to mix. Add the chicken strips, seal the bag, and shake vigorously to coat evenly with flour.
2. Put the egg and milk into a bowl and whisk together. Add the chicken strips, shaking off the excess flour as you remove them from the bag. Stir until the strips are completely coated in the egg.
3. Pour the breadcrumbs into a shallow dish. Use one hand to remove the chicken strips from the egg mixture, a few at a time, allowing the excess egg to drip off, and place in the dish of breadcrumbs. Use the other hand to coat the chicken in the breadcrumbs, pressing them in firmly. As they are breaded, place the strips on baking sheets or racks. When you have finished breading the chicken strips leave them to stand for 10–15 minutes before frying.
4. Heat enough oil for deep-frying in a large saucepan or deep-fryer to 180–190°C/350–375°F, or until a cube of bread browns in 30 seconds. Add the chicken and cook for 2–3 minutes on each side, or until golden brown and cooked through. Work in batches, draining on kitchen paper, and keep the cooked chicken fingers warm until you have finished cooking.

CHICKEN MEATBALL PASTA

Serves: 4

Prep: 25 mins, plus cooling

Cook: 40–45 mins

Ingredients

- 3 tbsp olive oil
- 1 red onion, chopped
- 400 g/14 oz skinless, boneless chicken breasts, chopped
- 55 g/2 oz fresh white breadcrumbs
- 2 tsp dried oregano
- 1 garlic clove, crushed
- 400 g/14 oz canned chopped tomatoes
- 1 tbsp sun-dried tomato paste
- 300 ml/10 fl oz water
- 225 g/8 oz dried spaghetti or linguine
- salt and pepper
- Parmesan cheese shavings, to serve

Method

1. Heat 1 tablespoon of the oil in a large frying pan and fry half the chopped onion for 5 minutes, until just softened. Leave to cool.
2. Place the chicken, breadcrumbs, oregano and the fried onion in a food processor. Season well with salt and pepper, and process for 2–3 minutes, until thoroughly combined. Shape into 24 meatballs.
3. Heat the remaining oil in the frying pan and fry the meatballs over a medium–high heat for 3–4 minutes, until golden brown. Remove and set aside.
4. Add the remaining onion and the garlic to the pan and fry for 5 minutes. Stir in the tomatoes, sun-dried tomato paste and water, and bring to the boil. Add the meatballs and simmer for 20 minutes until cooked through. Season to taste with salt and pepper.
5. Meanwhile, bring a large saucepan of lightly salted water to the boil. Add the pasta, bring back to the boil and cook for 8–10 minutes, until tender but still firm to the bite. Drain well and toss with the meatballs and sauce. Serve immediately with Parmesan cheese shavings.

CHICKEN KIEV

Makes: 8

Prep: 30 mins, plus chilling

Cook: 30 mins

Ingredients

- 115 g/4 oz butter, softened
- 3–4 garlic cloves, very finely chopped
- 1 tbsp chopped fresh parsley
- 1 tbsp snipped fresh chives
- juice and finely grated rind of ½ lemon
- 8 skinless, boneless chicken breasts, about 115 g/4 oz each
- 55 g/2 oz plain flour
- 2 eggs, lightly beaten
- 175 g/6 oz dry breadcrumbs
- groundnut oil or sunflower oil, for deep-frying
- salt and pepper
- cooked green vegetables, to serve

Method

1. Beat the butter in a bowl with the garlic, herbs, and lemon juice and rind. Season to taste with salt and pepper. Divide into eight pieces, then shape into cylinders. Wrap in foil and chill in the refrigerator until firm.
2. Place each chicken breast between two sheets of clingfilm and beat firmly with a meat mallet or rolling pin to flatten the chicken to an even thickness. Place a butter cylinder on each chicken piece and roll up. Secure with cocktail sticks.
3. Place the flour, eggs and breadcrumbs in separate shallow dishes. Dip the rolls into the flour, then the egg and, finally, the breadcrumbs. Chill in the refrigerator for 1 hour.
4. Heat enough oil for deep-frying in a saucepan or deep-fat fryer to 180–190°C/350–375°F, or until a cube of bread browns in 30 seconds. Deep-fry the chicken, in batches, for 8–10 minutes, until the chicken is cooked through and the juices run clear when a skewer is inserted into the thickest part of the meat. Drain on kitchen paper. Serve immediately with green vegetables.

CANNELLONI WITH CHICKEN & HAM

Serves: 4 **Prep: 20 mins** **Cook: 1¼–1½ hours**

Ingredients

1 tbsp olive oil, plus extra for brushing

1 small onion, finely chopped

175 g/6 oz fresh chicken mince

115 g/4 oz ham, finely chopped

70 g/2½ oz cream cheese with garlic and herbs

8 dried no-precook cannelloni tubes

4 tbsp grated Parmesan cheese

salt and pepper

Tomato sauce

25 g/1 oz butter

2 tbsp olive oil

1 onion, finely chopped

2 garlic cloves, finely chopped

1 celery stick, finely chopped

400 g/14 oz canned chopped tomatoes

2 tbsp tomato purée

brown sugar, to taste

1 tbsp chopped fresh flat-leaf parsley

100 ml/3½ fl oz water

salt and pepper

Method

1 First, make the sauce. Melt the butter with the oil in a saucepan. Add the onion, garlic and celery and cook over a low heat, stirring occasionally, for 5 minutes, until softened. Stir in the tomatoes, tomato purée, sugar to taste, parsley and water and season to taste with salt and pepper. Increase the heat to medium and bring to the boil, then reduce the heat and simmer, stirring occasionally, for 20–30 minutes, until thickened.

2 Meanwhile preheat the oven to 190°C/375°F/Gas Mark 5. Brush an ovenproof dish with oil. Heat the oil in a frying pan, add the onion and cook over a low heat, stirring occasionally, for 5 minutes, until softened. Add the chicken and cook, stirring frequently, for a further few minutes, until lightly browned. Remove the pan from the heat, stir in the ham and cream cheese and season to taste with salt and pepper.

3 Fill the cannelloni tubes with the chicken mixture and put them into the prepared dish. Pour the sauce over them, sprinkle with the Parmesan and bake in the preheated oven for 35–40 minutes until cooked through. Serve immediately.

CHICKEN FETTUCCINI ALFREDO

Serves: 4 **Prep: 20 mins** **Cook: 25 mins, plus standing**

Ingredients

- 500 ml/18 fl oz chicken stock
- 2 skinless, boneless chicken breasts
- 475 ml/17 oz double cream
- 4 cloves garlic, very finely minced
- 2 egg yolks
- 175 g/6 oz freshly grated Parmesan cheese, plus extra to garnish
- 25/1 oz g chopped Italian parsley
- salt and pepper
- 450 g/1 lb fettuccini

Method

1. Bring the chicken breasts and stock to a simmer in a small saucepan over medium heat. Cover, reduce the heat to low and simmer for 12 minutes until the chicken is cooked through and the juices run clear when a skewer is inserted into the thickest part of the meat. Turn off the heat and let sit in the hot stock for 15 minutes. When the chicken has cooled, cut into thin slices and reserve.
2. Bring the chicken stock back to a boil over high heat. Cook until the broth has reduced by half. Add the cream and garlic and when the mixture comes to a simmer, reduce the heat to low.
3. Beat the eggs in a small bowl. Slowly whisk in a quarter of the hot cream mixture. Turn off the heat and whisk the egg mixture into the cream sauce. Stir in half the Parmesan and the parsley. Season to taste and stir in the chicken.
4. Meanwhile, bring a large saucepan of lightly salted water to the boil, add the pasta, bring back to the boil and cook for 8–10 minutes, until tender but still firm to the bite. Drain well, quickly return to the pot and pour over the sauce. Stir well, cover, and let sit for 1 minute. Stir in the remaining Parmesan and let sit 1 more minute. Serve hot, topped with extra Parmesan to garnish.

CHICKEN NOODLE CASSEROLE

Serves: 6 **Prep: 25 mins** **Cook: 55 mins**

Ingredients

40 g/1½ oz butter

½ onion, finely diced

3 tbsp plain flour

850 ml/1½ pints milk

300 ml/10 fl oz canned condensed cream of mushroom soup

1 tsp salt

¼ tsp pepper

350 g/12 oz dried egg noodles

1 large cooked chicken, meat removed and shredded

115 g/4 oz frozen peas, thawed and drained

1 red pepper, deseeded and sliced

175 g/6 oz Cheddar cheese, coarsely grated

25 g/1 oz fresh white breadcrumbs

2 tbsp olive oil, plus extra for oiling

Method

1 Melt the butter in a medium-sized saucepan, then add the onion and sauté over a medium–low heat for about 4 minutes, or until translucent. Increase the heat to medium, add the flour and cook, stirring constantly, for a further 2 minutes. Slowly pour in 225 ml/8 fl oz of the milk, whisking constantly, and heat until simmering.

2 Add the remaining milk, the soup, salt and pepper. Cook, stirring occasionally, until the sauce thickens and is simmering. Remove from the heat and reserve.

3 Bring a saucepan of lightly salted water to the boil, add the noodles and cook for 1 minute less than instructed on the packet. Drain well and add to a large mixing bowl. Add the sauce, chicken, peas, pepper and about two thirds of the cheese. Mix with a spatula to combine.

4 Preheat oven to 180°C/350°F/Gas Mark 4. Oil a 23 x 33-cm/9 x 13-inch casserole dish. Pour the mixture into the prepared dish and top with the remaining cheese. Mix the breadcrumbs and oil together in a small bowl until combined, then sprinkle evenly over the casserole. Bake in the preheated oven for 35 minutes, or until heated through, brown and bubbling.

JERK CHICKEN BURGERS

Serves: 4

Prep: 25 mins

Cook: 15 mins, plus standing

Ingredients

1 tsp soft light brown sugar
1 tsp ground ginger
½ tsp ground allspice
½ tsp dried thyme
½–1 tsp cayenne pepper or chopped fresh jalapeño chilli
1 tbsp lime juice
2 garlic cloves, finely chopped
½ tsp salt
½ tsp pepper
450 g/1 lb fresh chicken mince
1 tbsp vegetable oil
1 red pepper or yellow pepper, deseeded and cut into large flat pieces
1 tsp olive oil
1 tsp red wine vinegar
4 onion rolls, split
lettuce leaves
salt and pepper

Method

1. Place the sugar, ginger, allspice, thyme, cayenne pepper, lime juice, garlic, the salt and pepper in a bowl and mix together. Add the chicken and gently mix to combine. Divide the mixture into four equal-sized portions and shape each portion into a patty.
2. Place a griddle pan over a medium–high heat and add the vegetable oil. Add the red pepper and cook for about 5 minutes, turning frequently, until blackened. Transfer to a bowl, cover with clingfilm or a plate and leave to steam for 5 minutes. Remove the skin and cut the flesh into strips. Toss with the olive oil, vinegar, and salt and pepper to taste.
3. Put the patties in the pan and cook, covered, for about 5 minutes on each side until brown and cooked through. Place the burgers in the rolls and top with the lettuce and peppers. Serve immediately.

CHICKEN LASAGNE

Serves: 4 **Prep: 25 mins** **Cook: 55 mins**

Ingredients

350 g/12 oz frozen chopped spinach, thawed and drained

½ tsp ground nutmeg

450 g/1 lb skiness, boneless cooked chicken, diced

4 sheets of no-precook lasagne verde

1½ tbsp cornflour

425 ml/15 fl oz milk

4 tbsp freshly grated Parmesan cheese

salt and pepper

Tomato sauce

400 g/14 oz canned chopped tomatoes

1 onion, finely chopped

1 garlic clove, crushed

150 ml/5 fl oz white wine

3 tbsp tomato purée

1 tsp dried oregano

salt and pepper

Method

1. Preheat the oven to 200°C/400°F/Gas Mark 6. To make the tomato sauce, place the tomatoes in a saucepan and stir in the onion, garlic, wine, tomato purée and oregano. Bring to the boil and simmer for 20 minutes, until thick. Season to taste with salt and pepper.
2. Drain the spinach again and pat dry on kitchen paper. Arrange the spinach in the base of a rectangular ovenproof dish. Sprinkle with the nutmeg and season to taste with salt and pepper.
3. Arrange the diced chicken over the spinach and spoon the tomato sauce over it. Arrange the lasagne sheets over the tomato sauce.
4. Blend the cornflour with a little of the milk to make a paste. Pour the remaining milk into a pan and stir in the cornflour paste. Heat gently, stirring constantly, for 2–3 minutes, until the sauce thickens. Season to taste with salt and pepper.
5. Spoon the sauce over the lasagne sheets to cover them completely and transfer the dish to a baking sheet. Sprinkle the grated cheese over the sauce and bake in the preheated oven for 25 minutes, until heated through, golden brown and bubbling. Serve immediately.

CHICKEN & SPICY TOMATO SAUCE PARCELS

Serves: 4 **Prep: 20 mins** **Cook: 1 hour–1 hour 10 mins**

Ingredients

4 skinless, boneless chicken breasts

4 fresh tarragon sprigs

Spicy tomato sauce

25 g/1 oz butter

2 tbsp olive oil

1 onion, finely chopped

2 garlic cloves, finely chopped

1 celery stick, finely chopped

2 orange peppers, deseeded and chopped

400 g/14 oz canned chopped tomatoes

2 tbsp sun-dried tomato paste

brown sugar, to taste

1 tbsp paprika

1 tsp chilli powder

1 tsp dried thyme

100 ml/3½ fl oz water

salt and pepper

Method

1 First, make the sauce. Melt the butter with the oil in a saucepan. Add the onion, garlic, celery and peppers and cook over a low heat, stirring occasionally, for 5 minutes, until softened. Stir in the tomatoes, sun-dried tomato paste, sugar to taste, paprika, chilli powder, thyme and water and season to taste with salt and pepper. Increase the heat to medium and bring to the boil, then reduce the heat and simmer, stirring occasionally, for 15–20 minutes, until thickened.

2 Meanwhile, preheat the oven to 190°C/375°F/Gas Mark 5. Cut four squares of greaseproof paper, each large enough to enclose a chicken breast. Put one chicken breast on each square.

3 Divide the sauce among the chicken fillets and top each with a tarragon sprig. Fold the paper over fairly loosely and double-fold the edges to seal. Put the parcels on a baking sheet and bake in the preheated oven for 35–40 minutes, until the chicken is cooked through and the juices run clear when a skewer is inserted into the thickest part of the meat. Serve immediately.

CHEDDAR & APPLE-STUFFED CHICKEN BREASTS

Serves: 4 **Prep: 20 mins** **Cook: 25–35 mins, plus standing**

Ingredients

4 thick skinless, boneless chicken breasts

6 slices Parma ham

salt and pepper

cooked green vegetables, to serve

Stuffing

1 tbsp sunflower oil, plus extra for oiling

1 small onion, finely chopped

1 celery stick, finely chopped

¼ tsp dried sage

1 eating apple, about 150 g/5½ oz, cored and diced

85 g/3 oz mature Cheddar cheese, coarsely grated

2 tbsp finely chopped parsley, plus extra to garnish

Method

1. Preheat the oven to 190°C/375°F/Gas Mark 5 and lightly oil a small roasting tin.
2. Put a chicken breast on a chopping board, rounded side up. Use a small, sharp knife to cut a pocket along the length of the breast, cutting as deep as you can without cutting through to the other side or the ends. Repeat with the remaining chicken breasts, then set aside.
3. To make the stuffing, heat the oil in a frying pan, add the onion, celery and sage and fry, stirring, for 3–5 minutes until soft. Stir in the apple and fry for a further 2 minutes until it is soft but not falling apart. Stir in the cheese and parsley and season with salt and pepper.
4. Divide the stuffing between the breast pockets. Wrap 1½ slices of ham around each breast, then rub the tops with a little oil.
5. Transfer to the prepared tin and roast in the preheated oven for 20–25 minutes, until the chicken is cooked through and the juices run clear when a skewer is inserted into the thickest part of the meat. Remove from the oven, cover with foil and leave to stand for 3–5 minutes before serving with green vegetables.

3
4

SOUTHERN-STYLE CHICKEN DRUMSTICKS

Serves: 4

Prep: 15 mins, plus chilling & cooling

Cook: 45–50 mins

Ingredients

8 chicken drumsticks
500 ml/18 fl oz milk
200 g/7 oz plain flour
1 tsp garlic salt
¼ tsp cayenne pepper
1 tbsp dried parsley
1 tsp dried thyme
1 large egg, beaten
sunflower oil, for deep-frying

Method

1 Place the drumsticks in a large bowl and pour over the milk. Cover and chill in the refrigerator for 1 hour.

2 Put the chicken and milk into a large saucepan and heat over a medium heat until boiling. Reduce the heat, cover and simmer gently for 20 minutes until the chicken is cooked. Drain well and leave to cool slightly.

3 Mix together the flour, garlic salt, cayenne pepper, parsley and thyme in a shallow bowl. Put the egg into a separate shallow bowl. Dip the chicken drumsticks in the seasoned flour to coat evenly. Dip into the beaten egg, then dip again into the seasoned flour.

4 Heat enough oil for deep-frying in a large saucepan or deep-fryer to 170°C/340°F, checking the temperature with a thermometer. Lower the chicken drumsticks into the oil and fry in batches for 6–8 minutes until the chicken is cooked through and the juices run clear when a skewer is inserted into the thickest part of the meat. Keep the cooked chicken warm while you cook the remaining drumsticks.

5 Remove the chicken with a slotted spoon, drain on absorbent kitchen paper and serve.

WHITE CHILLI

Serves: 4 **Prep: 15 mins** **Cook: 20-25 mins**

Ingredients

- 2 tbsp sunflower oil
- 450 g/1 lb fresh chicken mince
- 1 large onion, chopped
- 2 large garlic cloves, finely chopped
- 2 tsp dried oregano
- 1 tsp dried thyme
- 1 tsp ground coriander
- 1 tsp ground cumin
- ½ tsp cayenne pepper
- 400 g/14 oz canned cannellini beans
- 400 g/14 oz canned chopped tomatoes
- 125 ml/4 fl oz passata
- ½ tsp soft light brown sugar
- salt and pepper
- cooked rice and chopped fresh flat-leaf parsley, to serve

Method

1. Heat the oil in a saucepan over a medium–high heat. Add the chicken and onion and fry, stirring with a wooden spoon to break up the meat into large clumps, for 3–5 minutes until the onion is soft.
2. Add the garlic, oregano, thyme, coriander, cumin and cayenne pepper and fry for a further minute.
3. Drain and rinse the beans. Add to the pan with the tomatoes, passata and sugar and season to taste with salt and pepper. Bring to the boil, stirring. Reduce the heat to low, cover and simmer for 10–15 minutes until the chicken is cooked through. Adjust the seasoning, if necessary.
4. Divide the rice between four bowls, spoon over the chilli and sprinkle with parsley. Serve immediately.

CHICKEN, MUSHROOM & TARRAGON PIE

Serves: 4–6

Prep: 45 mins, plus chilling & cooling

Cook: 2 hours 20 mins

Ingredients

Filling

1 whole chicken, weighing 1.5 kg/3 lb 5 oz

2 fresh tarragon sprigs

1 Spanish onion, cut into wedges

300 ml/10 fl oz water

25 g/1 oz butter

175 g/6 oz chestnut mushrooms, sliced

2 tbsp plain flour

55 g/2 oz frozen or shelled fresh peas

1 tbsp chopped fresh tarragon

salt and pepper

Pastry

225 g/8 oz plain flour, plus extra for dusting

pinch of salt

175 g/6 oz butter

4 tbsp iced water

1 egg, lightly beaten

Method

1 Preheat the oven to 200°C/400°F/Gas Mark 6. Put the chicken, tarragon sprigs and onion into a casserole, add the water and season. Cover and bake for 1½ hours, until the chicken is cooked through and the juices run clear when a skewer is inserted into the thickest part of the meat. Remove the chicken. Strain the juices into a measuring jug and chill.

2 To make the pastry, sift the flour with the salt into a bowl and add the butter and water. Mix to a firm but slightly lumpy dough, adding more iced water if necessary. Roll out into a rectangle on a lightly floured surface, then fold the top third down and the bottom third up. Give the dough a quarter turn, roll out and fold again. Repeat once more, then wrap and chill for 30 minutes.

3 Discard the chicken skin, take the meat off the bones and dice. Skim off the fat from the cooking juices and make up to 300 ml/10 fl oz with water.

4 Melt the butter in a pan. Cook the mushrooms over a medium heat for 3 minutes. Stir in the flour for 1 minute, then gradually stir in the cooking juices. Bring to the boil, add the chicken, peas and tarragon and season to taste. Transfer to a large pie dish and cool.

5. Preheat the oven to 200°C/400°F/Gas Mark 6. Roll out the pastry to 2.5 cm/ 1 inch larger than the top of the dish. Cut out a 15-mm/⅝-inch strip all the way around. Brush the rim of the dish with water and press the strip on to it. Brush with water and lift the remaining dough on top. Trim off the excess and crimp the edges to seal. Make a slit in the centre and brush with beaten egg. Roll out the trimmings and use to decorate the pie, then brush with beaten egg. Bake for 40 minutes, until golden. Serve immediately.

CHICKEN RIGATONI BOLOGNESE

Serves: 6 **Prep: 15 mins** **Cook: 1 hour 15 mins, plus standing**

Ingredients

3 tbsp olive oil

1 onion, chopped

900 g/2 lb fresh chicken mince

4 garlic cloves, finely chopped

2 tsp dried mixed herbs, to taste

1 tsp salt, or to taste

90 ml/3 fl oz milk

900 g/2 lb ready-made tomato pasta sauce

450 ml/16 fl oz water, plus extra if needed

handful fresh flat-leaf parsley, chopped

450 g/1 lb dried rigatoni

pepper

freshly grated Parmesan cheese, to serve

Method

1. Heat the oil in a large saucepan, add the onion and chicken and sauté over a medium heat for about 10 minutes, using a wooden spoon to break up the chicken, until the onion is soft. Add the garlic, herbs, salt, pepper to taste and milk. Cook, stirring, for 2 minutes.
2. Add the pasta sauce, water and parsley. Simmer uncovered over a medium–low heat for 1 hour, until the chicken is cooked through. Add more water, if needed, to prevent the sauce becoming too thick.
3. Stir the pasta into the sauce, then remove from the heat. Cover and leave to stand for 2 minutes before serving. Serve with freshly grated Parmesan cheese.

FRIED CHICKEN WITH TOMATO & BACON SAUCE

Serves: 4 **Prep: 15 mins** **Cook: 35–45 mins**

Ingredients

25 g/1 oz butter
2 tbsp olive oil
4 skinless, boneless chicken breasts

Tomato & bacon sauce

25 g/1 oz butter
2 tbsp olive oil
1 large onion, finely chopped
2 garlic cloves, finely chopped
1 celery stick, finely chopped
4 rashers bacon, diced
400 g/14 oz canned chopped tomatoes
2 tbsp tomato purée
brown sugar, to taste
100 ml/3½ fl oz water
1 tbsp chopped fresh basil
1 tbsp chopped fresh flat-leaf parsley, plus extra to garnish
salt and pepper

Method

1. First, make the tomato and bacon sauce. Melt the butter with the oil in a large saucepan. Add the onion, garlic, celery and bacon and cook over a low heat, stirring occasionally, for 5 minutes, until softened. Stir in the tomatoes, tomato purée, sugar to taste and water and season to taste with salt and pepper. Increase the heat to medium and bring to the boil, then reduce the heat and simmer, stirring occasionally, for 15–20 minutes, until thickened.
2. Meanwhile, melt the butter with the oil in a large frying pan. Add the chicken and cook over a medium–high heat for 4–5 minutes on each side, until evenly browned.
3. Stir the basil and parsley into the sauce. Add the chicken and spoon the sauce over it. Cover and simmer for 10–15 minutes until the chicken is cooked through and the juices run clear when a skewer is inserted into the thickest part of the meat. Garnish with parsley and serve.

CHICKEN CARBONARA

Serves: 6 **Prep: 20 mins** **Cook: 20–25 mins**

Ingredients

- 1 tbsp olive oil
- 6 bacon rashers, chopped into small pieces
- 1 garlic clove, finely chopped
- 600 ml/1 pint double cream
- 100 g/3½ oz finely grated Parmesan cheese
- 6 egg yolks
- 40 g/1½ oz chopped fresh flat-leaf parsley
- 40 g/1½ oz chopped fresh basil
- 450 g/1 lb dried spaghetti
- 1 whole cooked chicken, weighing 1.5 kg/3 lb 5 oz, meat removed and shredded
- salt and pepper

Method

1. Heat the oil in a large, deep frying pan over a medium heat. Add the bacon and cook until almost crisp. Remove from the heat and spoon off all but 1 tablespoon of the fat.
2. In a mixing bowl, whisk together the garlic, cream, cheese, egg yolks, parsley and basil. Bring a large saucepan of lightly salted water to the boil, add the pasta, bring back to the boil and cook for 2 minutes less than instructed on the packet. Drain well.
3. Return the bacon pan to a medium–low heat, add the chicken and stir to combine. Add the hot spaghetti and the cream mixture and cook without boiling, tossing constantly, for 4–5 minutes, until the chicken is piping hot, the sauce has thickened slightly and the pasta is cooked. Reduce the heat if needed during this step.
4. Season the pasta with salt and pepper to taste and serve immediately.

★ Variation

For a simple variation add 85 g/3 oz cooked peas and 1 tablespoon of fresh mint.

WINTER WARMERS

RICH CHICKEN CASSEROLE 158
WINTER POT-ROAST CHICKEN 160
CHICKEN-STUFFED SQUASH 162
LEMON & HERB ROAST CHICKEN WITH WATERCRESS 164
CHICKEN WITH FORTY CLOVES OF GARLIC 166
HUNTER'S CHICKEN 168
CHICKEN IN WHITE WINE 169
CHICKEN IN TOMATO & ALMOND SAUCE 170
CHICKEN & DUMPLINGS 172
DEVILLED CHICKEN 174
CHICKEN CASSEROLE WITH A HERB CRUST 176
ROASTED CHICKEN AND RED POTATOES 178
CHICKEN THIGHS WITH SWEET-&-SOUR APRICOT SAUCE 179
CHICKEN WITH TOMATO & CINNAMON SAUCE 180
GREEK HERB ROAST CHICKEN 181
CHICKEN & AUBGERINE LAYERS BAKED IN TOMATO SAUCE 182
WHOLE ROAST GARLIC HERB CHICKEN WITH PAN GRAVY 184
CAJUN CHICKEN 186
CHICKEN & VEGETABLE BAKE 188
CHICKEN & ORZO BAKE 190
CHICKEN IN RIESLING 192
CHILLI VERDE CHICKEN STEW 194
SPICY AROMATIC CHICKEN 196
LOUISANA CHICKEN 197
SPICED CHICKEN STEW 198
CHICKEN & BROCCOLI CASSEROLE 200
CHICKEN TRAY BAKE 202
CHICKEN, PUMPKIN & CHORIZO CASSEROLE 204

RICH CHICKEN CASSEROLE

Serves: 4 **Prep:15 mins** **Cook: 1¼ hours**

Ingredients

- 2 tbsp olive oil
- 8 chicken thighs
- 1 medium red onion, sliced
- 2 garlic cloves, crushed
- 1 large red pepper, deseeded and thickly sliced
- thinly pared rind and juice of 1 small orange
- 125 ml/4 fl oz chicken stock
- 400 g/14 oz canned chopped tomatoes
- 25 g/1 oz sun-dried tomatoes, thinly sliced
- 1 tbsp chopped fresh thyme
- 50 g/1¾ oz pitted black olives
- salt and pepper
- thyme sprigs and orange rind, to garnish

Method

1. In a heavy or non-stick large frying pan, heat the oil and fry the chicken over a fairly high heat, turning occasionally until golden brown. Using a slotted spoon, drain off any excess fat from the chicken and transfer to a flameproof casserole.
2. Fry the onion, garlic and red pepper in the pan over a moderate heat for 3–4 minutes. Transfer the vegetables to the casserole.
3. Add the orange rind and juice, chicken stock, canned tomatoes and sun-dried tomatoes and stir to combine.
4. Bring to the boil then cover the casserole with a lid and simmer very gently over a low heat for about 1 hour, stirring occasionally until the chicken is cooked through and the juices run clear when a skewer is inserted into the thickest part of the meat. Add the thyme and olives, then adjust the seasoning with salt and pepper. Scatter over the thyme sprigs and orange rind to garnish and serve.

★ Variation

Add a mixture of dried herbs, such as oregano, thyme, basil and rosemary with the onion.

WINTER POT-ROAST CHICKEN

Serves: 4 **Prep: 15 mins** **Cook: 2 hours–2 hours 5 mins**

Ingredients

- 2 tbsp sunflower oil
- 25 g/1 oz butter
- 1 whole chicken, weighing 1.3 kg/3 lb
- 280 g/10 oz parsnips, diced
- 280 g/10 oz swede, diced
- 280 g/10 oz carrots, diced
- 6 shallots, halved
- 450 ml/16 fl oz chicken stock
- 40 g/1½ oz pearl barley
- 1 bouquet garni
- salt and pepper
- fresh thyme sprigs, to garnish

Method

1. Preheat the oven to 160°C/325°F/Gas Mark 3. Heat 1 tablespoon of the oil and the butter in a large frying pan. Season the chicken well with salt and pepper and fry in the hot fat, turning, for 7–8 minutes, until lightly browned. Transfer to a large casserole.
2. Add the remaining oil to the pan and stir in the diced vegetables and shallots. Fry over a medium–high heat, stirring, for 10 minutes. Add the stock and pearl barley, then bring to the boil. Simmer for 5 minutes, then transfer to the casserole dish. Add the bouquet garni and season to taste with salt and pepper.
3. Cover and cook in the preheated oven for 1 hour 15 minutes. Uncover the dish and cook for a further 20 minutes until the chicken is cooked through and the juices run clear when a skewer is inserted into the thickest part of the meat. Garnish with thyme sprigs and serve immediately.

2
2

CHICKEN-STUFFED SQUASH

Serves: 4

Prep: 25 mins, plus cooling

Cook: 55 mins

Ingredients

- 3 tbsp garlic-flavoured olive oil or plain olive oil
- 2 butternut squash, about 500 g/1 lb 2 oz each, halved lengthways, deseeded, all the fibres removed and the flesh slashed in a criss-cross pattern
- 450 g/1 lb fresh chicken mince
- 1 red onion, finely chopped
- ½ tsp dried red chilli flakes, or to taste
- 100 g/3½ oz baby spinach leaves
- freshly grated nutmeg, to taste
- 4 tbsp toasted pine nuts
- 100 g/3½ oz feta cheese, drained and crumbled
- 2 tbsp chopped fresh parsley
- salt and pepper
- salad leaves, to serve

Method

1. Preheat the oven to 200°C/400°F/Gas Mark 6. Rub 1 tablespoon of the oil over the squash halves, place them on a baking sheet, cut side up, and roast in the preheated oven for 45 minutes, or until tender.
2. Meanwhile, heat the remaining oil in a saucepan over a medium–high heat. Add the chicken, onion, chilli flakes, and salt and pepper to taste and fry, stirring with a wooden spoon to break up the chicken into large clumps, for 4–6 minutes until the chicken is cooked through.
3. Add the spinach and nutmeg, increase the heat and stir until the liquid from the spinach evaporates. Transfer to a bowl and set aside.
4. Remove the squash from the oven (do not switch off the oven) and leave until cool enough to handle.
5. Scoop out the squash flesh, retaining a thin shell. Finely chop the flesh and add to the bowl with the remaining ingredients. Toss together and adjust the seasoning, if necessary.
6. Divide the stuffing between the hollowed-out squash halves. Return to the oven for 10 minutes, or until heated through and the cheese is melted. Serve with salad leaves.

LEMON & HERB ROAST CHICKEN WITH WATERCRESS

Serves: 4 **Prep: 35 mins** **Cook: 1 hour 20 mins**

Ingredients

2 lemons, halved and juiced, halves reserved

4 fresh thyme sprigs

2 fresh rosemary sprigs

6 garlic cloves, unpeeled and crushed

1 whole chicken, weighing 1.8 kg/4 lb

1 onion, sliced

1 tbsp olive oil

125 ml/4 fl oz chicken stock

2 tbsp walnut oil or hazelnut oil

2 bunches watercress, stems removed

salt and pepper

Method

1. Preheat the oven to 200°C/400°F/Gas Mark 6. Put the lemon halves and juice, thyme, rosemary, garlic, and salt and pepper to taste into a large mixing bowl. Whisk together, then add the chicken, turning to coat on all sides. Fill the cavity with the contents of the bowl and tie the legs together with a piece of string.
2. Put the onion in the base of a 23 x 33-cm/ 9 x 13-inch metal or flameproof glass baking dish and place the chicken on top. Drizzle the chicken with olive oil, season generously with salt and roast in the preheated oven for 1 hour 15 minutes until the chicken is cooked through and the juices run clear when a skewer is inserted into the thickest part of the meat.
3. Transfer the chicken to a plate and cover with foil while you make the sauce. Add the chicken stock to the baking dish, scraping the base of the dish to deglaze any of the caramelized juices. Strain the liquid into a bowl, add the walnut oil and whisk to combine. Pour in any juices that have collected on the plate under the chicken. Add salt and pepper to taste.

4 To serve, toss the watercress in a large bowl with half the hot sauce to wilt it very slightly. Divide the watercress between four plates. Cut the chicken into serving portions and place on top of the watercress. Spoon over the remaining sauce and serve immediately.

CHICKEN WITH FORTY CLOVES OF GARLIC

Serves: 6 **Prep: 20 mins** **Cook: 1½–1¾ hours**

Ingredients

- 1 whole chicken, weighing 1.6 kg/3 lb 8 oz
- 3 garlic bulbs, separated into cloves but unpeeled
- 6 fresh thyme sprigs
- 2 fresh tarragon sprigs
- 2 bay leaves
- 300 ml/10 fl oz dry white wine
- salt and pepper

Method

1. Preheat the oven to 180°C/350°F/Gas Mark 4. Season the chicken inside and out with salt and pepper, then truss with kitchen string. Place on a rack in a casserole and arrange the garlic and herbs around it.
2. Pour the wine over the chicken and cover with a tight-fitting lid. Cook in the preheated oven for 1½–1¾ hours until the chicken is cooked through and the juices run clear when a skewer is inserted into the thickest part of the meat.
3. Remove and discard the bay leaves. Transfer the chicken and garlic to a dish and keep warm. Strain the cooking juices into a jug. Skim off any fat on the surface of the cooking juices.
4. Carve the chicken and transfer to serving plates with the garlic. Spoon over a little of the cooking juices and serve immediately.

1
2

HUNTER'S CHICKEN

Serves: 4 **Prep: 15 mins** **Cook: 1 hour 25 mins**

Ingredients

15 g/½ oz unsalted butter

2 tbsp olive oil

1.8 kg/4 lb skinless chicken pieces

2 red onions, sliced

2 garlic cloves, finely chopped

400 g/14 oz canned chopped tomatoes

2 tbsp chopped fresh flat-leaf parsley

6 fresh basil leaves, torn

1 tbsp sun-dried tomato purée

150 ml/5 fl oz red wine

225 g/8 oz mushrooms, sliced

salt and pepper

Method

1. Preheat the oven to 160°C/325°F/Gas Mark 3. Heat the butter and oil in a flameproof casserole and cook the chicken over a medium–high heat, turning frequently, for 10 minutes, or until golden all over and sealed. Using a slotted spoon, transfer to a plate.
2. Add the onions and garlic to the casserole and cook over a low heat, stirring occasionally, for 10 minutes, or until softened and golden. Add the tomatoes with their juice, the herbs, sun-dried tomato purée and wine, and season to taste with salt and pepper. Bring to the boil, then return the chicken portions to the casserole, pushing them down into the sauce.
3. Cover and cook in the preheated oven for 50 minutes. Add the mushrooms and cook for a further 10 minutes, until the chicken is cooked through and the juices run clear when a skewer is inserted into the thickest part of the meat. Serve immediately.

CHICKEN IN WHITE WINE

Serves: 4 **Prep: 20 mins** **Cook: 1 hour 50 mins–1 hour 55 mins**

Ingredients

- 55 g/2 oz butter
- 2 tbsp olive oil
- 2 rindless, thick streaky bacon rashers, chopped
- 115 g/4 oz baby onions, peeled
- 1 garlic clove, finely chopped
- 1.8 kg/4 lb chicken pieces
- 400 ml/14 fl oz dry white wine
- 300 ml/10 fl oz chicken stock
- 1 bouquet garni
- 115 g/4 oz button mushrooms
- 25 g/1 oz plain flour
- salt and pepper
- fresh mixed herbs, to garnish

Method

1 Preheat the oven to 160°C/325°F/Gas Mark 3. Melt half the butter with the oil in a flameproof casserole. Add the bacon and cook over a medium heat, stirring, for 5–10 minutes, or until golden brown. Transfer the bacon to a large plate. Add the onions and garlic to the casserole and cook over a low heat, stirring occasionally, for 10 minutes, or until golden. Transfer to the plate. Add the chicken and cook over a medium heat, stirring constantly, for 8–10 minutes, or until golden. Transfer to the plate.

2 Drain off any excess fat from the casserole. Stir in the wine and stock and bring to the boil, scraping any sediment off the base. Add the bouquet garni and season to taste. Return the bacon, onions and chicken to the casserole. Cover and cook in the preheated oven for 1 hour, until the chicken is cooked through and the juices run clear when a skewer is inserted into the thickest part of the meat. Add the mushrooms, re-cover and cook for 15 minutes. Meanwhile, make a beurre manié by mashing the remaining butter with the flour.

3 Set the casserole over a medium heat and discard the bouquet garni. Whisk in the beurre manié, a little at a time. Bring to the boil, stirring constantly, then serve, garnished with fresh herbs.

CHICKEN IN TOMATO & ALMOND SAUCE

Serves: 4 **Prep: 20 mins** **Cook: 40 mins**

Ingredients

- 25 g/1 oz butter
- 2 tbsp olive oil
- 2 shallots, finely chopped
- 3 garlic cloves, finely chopped
- 1 celery stick, finely chopped
- 55 g/2 oz ground almonds
- 4 tbsp fresh breadcrumbs
- 3 tbsp chopped fresh flat-leaf parsley, plus extra to garnish
- 500 g/1 lb 2 oz plum tomatoes, peeled, cored and chopped
- 2 tbsp tomato purée
- brown sugar, to taste
- 4 skinless, boneless chicken breasts
- 1 litre/1¾ pints hot chicken stock
- juice of ½ orange
- 1 bouquet garni
- 6 black peppercorns
- 2 tbsp flaked almonds
- salt and pepper

Method

1. Melt the butter with the oil in a saucepan. Add the shallots, garlic and celery and cook over a low heat, stirring occasionally, for 5 minutes, until softened. Remove the pan from the heat and stir in the ground almonds, breadcrumbs, parsley, tomatoes, tomato purée and sugar to taste. Season to taste with salt and pepper. Return the pan to the heat and cook, stirring constantly, for 5 minutes, or until thickened. Remove the pan from the heat.

2. Put the chicken into a large, shallow pan. Pour in the hot stock and orange juice, add the bouquet garni and peppercorns and bring just to the boil. Reduce the heat so that the water is barely shivering, cover and poach for 20 minutes, until the chicken is cooked through and the juices run clear when a skewer is inserted into the thickest part of the meat.

3. Transfer the chicken to a warmed serving dish and keep warm. Strain and reserve 5 tablespoons of the cooking liquid, then stir it into the sauce. Return the pan to the heat and cook, stirring constantly, until thoroughly combined and heated through. Pour the sauce over the chicken and sprinkle with the flaked almonds. Garnish with parsley and serve immediately.

CHICKEN & DUMPLINGS

Serves: 6

Prep: 30 mins, plus cooling

Cook: 1 hour 40 mins

Ingredients

2 tbsp vegetable oil

1 whole chicken, weighing 1.8 kg/4 lb, cut into quarters

1.2 litres/2 pints chicken stock

700 ml/1¼ pints water

4 garlic cloves, peeled

1 bay leaf

4 fresh thyme sprigs

55 g/2 oz butter

2 carrots, cut into 1-cm/½-inch pieces

2 celery sticks, cut into 1-cm/½-inch pieces

1 large onion, chopped

5 tbsp plain flour

salt and pepper

Dumplings

225 g/8 oz plain flour

2 tsp baking powder

¼ tsp bicarbonate of soda

35 g/1¼ oz chilled butter

2 spring onions, green parts only, thinly sliced

60 ml/2 fl oz buttermilk

175 ml/6 fl oz milk

Method

1 Place a large, heavy-based saucepan over a high heat and add the oil. Add the chicken pieces and brown all over. Add the stock, water, garlic, bay leaf and thyme and bring to the boil, then reduce the heat to low and simmer, covered, for 30 minutes, until the chicken is cooked through and the juices run clear when a skewer is inserted into the thickest part of the meat. Skim off any foam that comes to the surface.

2 Carefully remove the chicken from the pan and transfer to a bowl to cool. Strain the liquid into another bowl and reserve. Skim off any fat that comes to the top.

3 Return the pan to a medium heat and add the butter, carrots, celery and onion. Sauté the vegetables in the butter for 5 minutes. Add the flour and cook, stirring, for about 2 minutes. Gradually whisk in the reserved liquid. Season with salt and pepper to taste. Heat until simmering, stirring occasionally. Reduce the heat to low, and simmer, covered, for about 30 minutes, or until the vegetables are tender.

4 Meanwhile, remove all the cooled chicken meat from the bones, and tear into large chunks. When the vegetables are cooked, stir in the

chicken. Taste and adjust the seasoning if needed. Cover and reduce the heat to low.

5 To make the dumplings, put the flour, 1 teaspoon of salt, baking powder and bicarbonate of soda into a mixing bowl. Stir with a whisk to combine. Add the butter, cutting it in with a pastry knife until coarse crumbs form. Add the spring onions, buttermilk and milk, lightly stirring with a fork to make a thick, sticky dough.

6 Increase the heat under the pan to medium. As soon as the mixture is simmering, stir well, then drop large, rounded tablespoons of the dumpling dough into the simmering chicken mixture. Cover and cook for 15 minutes until the dumplings are firm and cooked in the middle, and the chicken is piping hot. Remove from the heat, uncover and serve hot.

DEVILLED CHICKEN

Serves: 4

Prep: 25 mins,
plus cooling

Cook: 2 hours 5 mins–
2 hours 10 mins

Ingredients

- 1 whole chicken, weighing 2.25 kg/5 lb
- 2 carrots, cut into chunks
- 1 celery stick, cut into lengths
- 6 black peppercorns
- 1 bouquet garni
- pinch of salt
- 25 g/1 oz butter, melted
- fresh thyme leaves, to garnish

Devil sauce

- 25 g/1 oz butter
- 2 tbsp olive oil
- 2 shallots, finely chopped
- 2 garlic cloves, finely chopped
- 1 celery stick, finely chopped
- 400 g/14 oz canned chopped tomatoes
- 2 tbsp tomato purée
- brown sugar, to taste
- 3 tbsp Worcestershire sauce
- 1 tbsp lemon juice
- 2 tbsp tarragon vinegar
- 1 bay leaf
- salt and pepper

Method

1. Put the chicken, carrots, celery, peppercorns, bouquet garni and salt into a large saucepan and pour in water to cover. Bring to the boil over a high heat, then reduce the heat, cover and simmer for 1½ hours, until the chicken is cooked through and juices run clear when a skewer is inserted into the thickest part of the meat. Remove from the heat and leave to cool.

2. Meanwhile, make the sauce. Melt the butter with the oil in a saucepan. Add the shallots, garlic and celery and cook over a low heat, stirring occasionally, for 5 minutes, until softened. Stir in the tomatoes, tomato purée, sugar to taste, Worcestershire sauce, lemon juice, vinegar and bay leaf and season to taste with salt and pepper. Increase the heat to medium and bring to the boil, then reduce the heat and simmer, stirring occasionally, for 15–20 minutes, until thickened.

3. Preheat the grill. Remove the chicken from the pan and strain the cooking liquid into a bowl. Remove and discard the skin, cut the chicken into eight pieces and put them into a flameproof casserole. Brush the chicken with the melted butter and cook under the preheated grill for 8 minutes on each side, until evenly browned.

4 Remove and discard the bay leaf from the sauce and stir in 300 ml/10 fl oz of the reserved cooking liquid. Pour the sauce over the chicken and cook over a medium heat for 10–15 minutes, until the chicken is heated through. Garnish with thyme and serve immediately.

CHICKEN CASSEROLE WITH A HERB CRUST

Serves: 4 **Prep: 20 mins** **Cook: 1 hour 40 mins**

Ingredients

4 chicken legs
2 tbsp plain flour
15 g/½ oz butter
1 tbsp olive oil
1 onion, chopped
3 garlic cloves, sliced
4 parsnips, cut into large chunks
150 ml/5 fl oz dry white wine
850 ml/1½ pints chicken stock
3 leeks, white parts only, sliced
75 g/2¾ oz prunes, halved (optional)
1 tbsp English mustard
1 bouquet garni
100 g/3½ oz fresh breadcrumbs
75 g/2¾ oz Caerphilly cheese, crumbled
50 g/1¾ oz mixed fresh tarragon and flat-leaf parsley, chopped
salt and pepper

Method

1. Preheat the oven to 180°C/350°F/Gas Mark 4. Toss the chicken legs in the flour, shaking off any excess. Melt the butter with the oil in a flameproof casserole. Add the chicken and fry, turning occasionally, until golden brown all over. Remove with a slotted spoon and keep warm.
2. Add the onion, garlic and parsnips to the casserole and cook for 20 minutes, or until the mixture is golden brown.
3. Add the wine, stock, leeks, prunes, if using, mustard and bouquet garni and season.
4. Return the chicken to the casserole, cover and cook in the preheated oven for 1 hour. Meanwhile, mix together the breadcrumbs, cheese and herbs.
5. Remove the casserole from the oven and increase the temperature to 200°C/400°F/ Gas Mark 6.
6. Remove the lid of the casserole and sprinkle over the crust mixture. Return the casserole to the oven, uncovered, for 10 minutes, until the crust starts to brown slightly, the chicken is cooked through and the juices run clear when a skewer is inserted into the thickest part of the meat. Serve immediately.

ROASTED CHICKEN & RED POTATOES

Serves: 4 **Prep: 25 mins** **Cook: 45 mins**

Ingredients

60 ml/2 fl oz olive oil
2 garlic cloves, finely chopped
2 tbsp chopped fresh flat-leaf parsley
1 tsp dried rosemary
1 tsp dried thyme
1 tsp Dijon mustard
pinch of cayenne pepper
1 onion, thinly sliced
1 whole chicken, cut into 8 pieces
1.2 kg/2 lb 8 oz small red potatoes, washed but not peeled
2 tbsp sherry vinegar
salt and pepper

Method

1. Preheat the oven to 220°C/425°F/Gas Mark 7.
2. Put the oil, garlic, parsley, rosemary, thyme, mustard and cayenne pepper into a mixing bowl and whisk to combine.
3. Place the onion, chicken and potatoes into a large roasting tin. Pour over the herb mixture, and use your hands to toss everything together. Space the chicken pieces as far apart as possible.
4. Generously season the contents of the tin with salt and pepper. Roast in the preheated oven for 45 minutes, or until the potatoes are tender, the chicken is cooked through and the juices run clear when a skewer is inserted into the thickest part of the meat. Transfer the chicken to a serving platter.
5. Add the vinegar to the tin and use a spatula to toss everything together. Add the potato mixture to the platter of chicken and serve immediately.

CHICKEN THIGHS WITH SWEET-&-SOUR APRICOT SAUCE

Serves: 8 **Prep: 15 mins** **Cook: 1 hour 25 mins, plus resting**

Ingredients

8 chicken thighs
1 tbsp olive oil
1 onion, sliced
1 carrot, sliced
1 celery stick, sliced
6 garlic cloves, bruised
6 fresh thyme sprigs
25 ml/8 fl oz chicken stock
salt and pepper

Apricot sauce

325 g/11½ oz apricot jam
2 tbsp rice wine vinegar
1 tbsp fresh thyme leaves

Method

1. Preheat oven to 160°C/325°F/Gas Mark 3.
2. Generously season the chicken thighs all over with salt and pepper. Heat the oil in a large, ovenproof frying pan over a medium heat and add the chicken, skin side down. Cook for about 5 minutes until the skin is well browned. Turn and cook on the other side for 3 minutes.
3. Transfer to a plate, pour off the excess fat and add the onion, carrot, celery, garlic and thyme to the pan. Arrange the chicken on top of the vegetables, skin side up. Pour in the stock and cover with foil.
4. Roast in the preheated oven for 1 hour, or until the meat is almost fork tender. Uncover and increase the oven temperature to 220°C/425°F/Gas Mark 7. Roast for a further 10 minutes until the chicken is cooked through and the juices run clear when a skewer is inserted into the thickest part of the meat. Remove from the oven and leave to rest for 10 minutes before serving.
5. Meanwhile, make the apricot sauce. Put the jam, vinegar and 1 tablespoon of water in a small saucepan over a medium heat. Heat, stirring, until simmering. Remove from the heat and stir in the thyme, and salt and pepper to taste. Serve warm, spooned over the chicken.

CHICKEN WITH TOMATO & CINNAMON SAUCE

Serves: 4 **Prep: 15 mins** **Cook: 1 hour 5 mins**

Ingredients

55 g/2 oz butter
2 tbsp olive oil
4 chicken quarters
1 onion, finely chopped
2 garlic cloves, finely chopped
1 celery stick, finely chopped
400 g/14 oz canned chopped tomatoes
2 tbsp tomato purée
1 tsp Dijon mustard
brown sugar, to taste
2 tbsp lemon juice
3 tbsp chicken stock
1 tsp dried oregano
¾ tsp ground cinnamon
salt and pepper

Method

1 Melt the butter with the oil in a flameproof casserole. Season the chicken well with salt and pepper, add to the casserole and cook over a medium heat, turning frequently, for 8–10 minutes, until evenly browned. Remove from the casserole and set aside.

2 Add the onion, garlic and celery to the casserole and cook over a low heat, stirring occasionally, for 5 minutes, until softened. Stir in the tomatoes, tomato purée, mustard, sugar to taste, lemon juice, stock, oregano and cinnamon and season to taste with salt and pepper. Increase the heat to medium and bring to the boil, then reduce the heat and simmer, stirring occasionally, for 15 minutes.

3 Return the chicken to the casserole and spoon the sauce over it. Cover and simmer, stirring occasionally, for 30 minutes, until the chicken is cooked through and the juices run clear when a skewer is inserted into the thickest part of the meat. Serve immediately.

GREEK HERB ROAST CHICKEN

Serves: 4

Prep: 20 mins, plus marinating

Cook: 45 mins, plus resting

Ingredients

- 125 ml/4 fl oz olive oil
- 3 garlic cloves, chopped
- 1 tbsp chopped fresh rosemary
- 1 tbsp chopped fresh thyme
- 1 tbsp chopped fresh oregano
- 1 tbsp chopped fresh marjoram
- juice of 2 lemons
- 1 whole chicken, weighing 1.8 kg/4 lb, cut into pieces
- salt and pepper

Method

1. In a large glass baking dish, mix the oil, garlic, rosemary, thyme, oregano, marjoram and lemon juice together. Add the chicken pieces, season to taste with salt and pepper and toss well. Tightly wrap in clingfilm and marinate overnight in the refrigerator.
2. Preheat the oven to 220°C/425°F/Gas Mark 7.
3. Roast the chicken in the preheated oven for 45 minutes, until the chicken is cooked through and the juices run clear when a skewer is inserted into the thickest part of the meat. Remove from the oven and leave to rest for 5 minutes. Serve immediately with any cooking juices spooned over the top.

CHICKEN & AUBERGINE LAYERS BAKED IN TOMATO SAUCE

Serves: 4 **Prep: 30 mins** **Cook: 50–55 mins**

Ingredients

- 4 skinless, boneless chicken breasts
- 2 aubergines, sliced
- 4 tbsp plain flour
- 275 ml/9½ fl oz olive oil
- 55 g/2 oz dry breadcrumbs
- 1 egg
- 55 g/2 oz Parmesan cheese, grated
- chopped fresh flat-leaf parsley, to garnish

Tomato sauce

- 25 g/1 oz butter
- 2 tbsp olive oil
- 1 onion, finely chopped
- 2 garlic cloves, finely chopped
- 1 celery stick, finely chopped
- 400 g/14 oz canned chopped tomatoes
- 2 tbsp tomato purée
- 6 stoned olives, sliced
- brown sugar, to taste
- 1 tsp dried oregano
- 100 ml/3½ fl oz water
- salt and pepper

Method

1. Put the chicken between two sheets of clingfilm and beat until thin and even. Cut into 10-cm/4-inch pieces and set aside.
2. To make the sauce, melt the butter with the oil in a saucepan. Add the onion, garlic and celery and cook over a low heat, stirring occasionally, for 5 minutes, until softened. Stir in the tomatoes, tomato purée, olives, sugar to taste, oregano and water and season to taste with salt and pepper. Increase the heat to medium and bring to the boil, then reduce the heat and simmer, stirring occasionally, for 15–20 minutes, until thickened.
3. Meanwhile, dip the aubergine slices in the flour to coat. Heat 5 tablespoons of the oil in a large frying pan and cook the aubergine slices, in batches, for 3 minutes on each side, until lightly browned, adding more oil as necessary.
4. Preheat the oven to 180°C/350°F/Gas Mark 4. Spread out the breadcrumbs in a shallow dish and lightly beat the egg in a separate shallow dish. Dip the chicken first in the egg and then in the breadcrumbs to coat. Heat the remaining oil in the frying pan. Add the chicken and cook over a medium heat for 2 minutes on each side, until golden.

5 Layer the chicken and aubergine slices in an ovenproof dish, pour over the sauce and sprinkle with the Parmesan. Bake in the preheated oven for 20 minutes, until the chicken is cooked through and the juices run clear when a skewer is inserted into the thickest part of the meat. Garnish with parsley and serve immediately.

WHOLE ROAST GARLIC HERB CHICKEN WITH PAN GRAVY

Serves: 4

Prep: 25 mins, plus marinating

Cook: 1 hour 55 mins

Ingredients

4 garlic cloves, peeled, crushed and finely chopped

150 ml/5 fl oz olive oil

2 tsp very finely chopped fresh thyme

2 tsp very finely chopped fresh rosemary

1 tsp dried mixed herbs

1 whole chicken, weighing 2.25 kg/5 lb

salt and pepper

Gravy

1½ tbsp reserved chicken fat

1 tbsp butter

1 rounded tbsp flour

450 ml/16 fl oz chicken stock

½ tsp balsamic vinegar

4 fresh thyme sprigs

salt and pepper

Method

1. Preheat the oven to 230°C/450°F/Gas Mark 8.
2. Grind the garlic to a very fine paste in a mortar with a pestle.
3. Put the oil, garlic, thyme, rosemary and mixed herbs in a large bowl. Rub the chicken inside and out with the mixture. Leave to marinate for several hours or overnight.
4. Place the chicken in a roasting tin suitable for use on the hob. Season the cavity with salt and pepper. Truss the legs with kitchen string.
5. Roast in the preheated oven for 1 hour 40 minutes, until the chicken is cooked through and the juices run clear when a skewer is inserted into the thickest part of the meat. Remove the chicken from the oven, place on a warmed serving platter and cover with foil.
6. Meanwhile, make the gravy. Pour off the excess chicken fat, leaving 1½ tablespoons in the tin, then place over a medium heat and add the butter. When the butter is melted add the flour and cook, stirring constantly with a whisk, until golden brown. Whisk in the stock, vinegar and thyme. Increase the heat to high, bring to the boil and cook for 5 minutes, stirring, until the gravy is thickened. Serve with the chicken.

CAJUN CHICKEN

Serves: 4

Prep: 15 mins

Cook: 1 hour 5 mins–1 hour 10 mins

Ingredients

- 5 tbsp olive oil
- 4 skinless, boneless chicken breasts
- 55 g/2 oz plain flour
- 1 onion, finely chopped
- 2 garlic cloves, finely chopped
- 1 celery stick, finely chopped
- 1 green pepper, deseeded and chopped
- ½ tsp dried oregano
- ½ tsp dried thyme
- 1 bay leaf
- 2 fresh red chillies, deseeded and chopped
- 400 g/14 oz canned chopped tomatoes
- 2 tbsp tomato purée
- brown sugar, to taste
- 300 ml/10 fl oz chicken stock
- dash of hot pepper sauce (optional)
- salt and pepper

Method

1. Heat the oil in a flameproof casserole. Add the chicken and cook over a medium heat, for 3–5 minutes on each side, until evenly browned. Remove and set aside.
2. Reduce the heat to low, stir in half the flour and cook, stirring constantly, for 1 minute, then stir in the remaining flour. Cook, stirring constantly, until the mixture is the colour of peanut butter. Immediately add the onion, garlic, celery and green pepper and cook, stirring constantly, for 4 minutes. Add the oregano, thyme, bay leaf and chillies and cook, stirring, for a further minute, then remove the casserole from the heat and stir in the tomatoes, tomato purée and sugar to taste. Season to taste with salt and pepper.
3. Return the casserole to the heat and gradually stir in the stock. Bring to the boil, stirring constantly, then return the chicken to the casserole. Reduce the heat, cover and simmer, stirring occasionally, for 45 minutes, until the chicken is cooked through and the juices run clear when a skewer is inserted into the thickest part of the meat. Remove and discard the bay leaf. Stir in the hot pepper sauce if using and serve immediately.

CHICKEN & VEGETABLE BAKE

Serves: 4 **Prep: 20 mins** **Cook: 40–45 mins**

Ingredients

- 3 tbsp olive oil
- 2 leeks, sliced
- 2 garlic cloves, sliced
- 2 large skinless, boneless chicken breasts, chopped
- 2 sweet potatoes, peeled and cut into chunks
- 2 parsnips, scrubbed and sliced
- 1 red pepper, deseeded and cut into strips
- 1 yellow pepper, deseeded and cut into strips
- 250 g/9 oz mixed wild mushrooms, cleaned
- 400 g/14 oz tomatoes, roughly chopped
- 300 g/10½ oz cooked white long-grain rice
- 1 small bunch fresh parsley, chopped
- 125 g/4½ oz mature Cheddar cheese, grated
- salt and pepper

Method

1. Preheat the oven to 180°C/350°F/Gas Mark 4.
2. Heat the oil in a large frying pan over a medium heat, add the leeks and garlic and cook, stirring frequently, for 3–4 minutes until softened. Add the chicken and cook, stirring frequently, for 5 minutes. Add the sweet potatoes and parsnips and cook, stirring frequently, for 5 minutes, or until golden and beginning to soften. Add the peppers and mushrooms and cook, stirring frequently, for 5 minutes. Stir in the tomatoes, rice and parsley and season to taste with salt and pepper.
3. Spoon the mixture into an ovenproof dish, scatter over the Cheddar cheese and bake in the preheated oven for 20–25 minutes until the chicken is tender and cooked through. Serve.

CHICKEN & ORZO BAKE

Serves: 4 **Prep: 20 mins** **Cook: 45–50 mins**

Ingredients

- 100 g/3½ oz ricotta cheese, drained
- 125 g/4½ oz mozzarella cheese, drained and grated
- 55 g/2 oz Gruyère cheese, finely grated
- 125 g/4½ oz dried orzo pasta
- 2 tbsp olive oil, plus extra for oiling and drizzling
- 1 large onion, finely chopped
- 450 g/1 lb fresh chicken mince
- 4 large garlic cloves, finely chopped
- 1 tbsp dried mixed herbs
- 500 ml/18 fl oz passata
- 40 g/1½ oz fine dried breadcrumbs
- salt and pepper

Method

1. Preheat the oven to 220°C/425°F/Gas Mark 7 and oil a 1.2-litre/2-pint ovenproof serving dish. Beat together the ricotta cheese, mozzarella cheese and half the Gruyère cheese in a large bowl and set aside.
2. Bring a saucepan of lightly salted water to the boil. Add the pasta, bring back to the boil and cook for 2 minutes less than specified in the packet instructions.
3. Meanwhile, heat the oil in a frying pan over a medium–high heat. Add the onion and fry, stirring, for 2–3 minutes until soft. Add the chicken, garlic and herbs, stirring for about 2 minutes. Stir in the passata, season with salt and pepper, bring to the boil, then simmer for 10 minutes.
4. Drain the pasta and immediately tip it into the bowl with the cheese. Add the chicken mixture, stirring until the cheeses melt.
5. Pour into the prepared dish and smooth the surface. Combine the remaining Gruyère cheese with the breadcrumbs and sprinkle over the top, then drizzle with oil. Bake in the preheated oven for 20–25 minutes until the top is golden brown and bubbling and the chicken is cooked through. Serve immediately.

CHICKEN IN RIESLING

Serves: 4–6 **Prep: 30 mins** **Cook: 50 mins–1 hour**

Ingredients

- 1 whole chicken, weighing 1.6 kg/3 lb 8 oz, cut into 8 pieces
- 2 tbsp plain flour, seasoned with salt and pepper
- 55 g/2 oz butter, plus extra for the pasta
- 1 tbsp sunflower oil, plus extra if needed
- 4 shallots, finely chopped
- 400 g/14 oz chestnut mushrooms, sliced
- 2 tbsp brandy
- 300 ml/10 fl oz Riesling wine
- 2 carrots, thinly sliced
- 200 g/7 oz dried ribbon pasta, such as pappardelle or tagliatelle
- 100 ml/3½ fl oz crème fraîche or double cream
- salt and pepper

Method

1 Coat the chicken pieces with the seasoned flour, shaking off any excess, and set aside. Melt 25 g/1 oz of the butter with the oil in a flameproof casserole over a medium heat. Add the chicken pieces to the casserole and fry for 3–5 minutes until golden brown, removing each piece when it is browned and adding extra oil, if necessary. Wipe out the casserole.

2 Melt the remaining butter in the casserole. Add the shallots and fry, stirring, for 2–3 minutes, or until soft. Add the mushrooms and a pinch of salt and continue frying until they absorb the liquid they give off. Return the chicken to the casserole. Light the brandy in a ladle and pour over the chicken.

3 When the flames have died down, add the wine and carrots and enough water to cover all the ingredients. Bring to the boil, then reduce the heat to low and simmer for 20–25 minutes, until the chicken is cooked through and the juices run clear when a skewer is inserted into the thickest part of the meat. Preheat the oven to 110°C/225°F/Gas Mark ¼.

4 Meanwhile bring a large, heavy-based saucepan of lightly salted water to the boil. Add the pappardelle, bring back to the boil and cook for 8–10 minutes, or until just tender but still firm to the bite. Drain well, toss with butter and keep warm in the preheated oven. Using tongs and a slotted spoon transfer the chicken and the vegetables to a serving platter and keep warm in the oven. Skim any fat off the cooking juices, stir in the crème fraîche and bring to the boil, stirring, for 2–3 minutes to reduce. Taste and adjust the seasoning, if necessary, then pour the sauce over the chicken. Serve with the pasta.

CHILLI VERDE CHICKEN STEW

Serves: 4 **Prep: 25 mins** **Cook: 1 hour 25 mins**

Ingredients

2 tbsp vegetable oil

1 whole chicken, cut into 8 pieces

1 onion, diced

8–10 tomatillos, husk removed and quartered

2 jalapeño peppers, deseeded and chopped

6 garlic cloves, peeled

½ bunch fresh coriander, chopped

700 ml/1¼ pints chicken stock

2 tbsp ground cumin

2 tsp dried oregano

1 bay leaf

675 g/1 lb 8 oz potatoes, cut into large chunks

salt and pepper

soured cream, to serve (optional)

Method

1 Put the oil in a large, heavy-based saucepan and place over a medium–high heat. Season the chicken with salt and pepper, add to the pan and brown all over. Remove the chicken, reduce the heat to medium, and add the onion. Sauté for about 5 minutes until soft.

2 Meanwhile, add the tomatillos, jalapeños, garlic, coriander and stock to a blender and purée. Return the chicken to the pan, pour over the tomatillo mixture and stir in the cumin, oregano and bay leaf. Heat until simmering, then reduce the heat to medium–low, cover and simmer for 40 minutes, stirring occasionally.

3 Add the potatoes, pushing the chunks under the liquid so that they cook evenly. Cover and cook for a further 30 minutes, or until the potatoes are tender, the chicken is cooked through and the juices run clear when a skewer is inserted into the thickest part of the meat. Remove and discard the bay leaf. Serve hot in warmed bowls with a dollop of soured cream, if using.

SPICY AROMATIC CHICKEN

Serves: 4 **Prep: 15 mins** **Cook: 1 hour–1 hour 20 mins**

Ingredients

- 4 skinless chicken pieces
- ½ lemon, cut into wedges
- 4 tbsp olive oil
- 1 onion, roughly chopped
- 2 large garlic cloves, finely chopped
- 125 ml/4 fl oz dry white wine
- 400 g/14 oz canned chopped tomatoes in juice
- pinch of sugar
- ½ tsp ground cinnamon
- ½ tsp ground cloves
- ½ tsp ground allspice
- 400g/14 oz canned artichoke hearts or okra, drained
- 8 black olives, stoned
- salt and pepper

Method

1 Rub the chicken pieces with the lemon. Heat the oil in a large flameproof casserole or lidded frying pan. Add the onion and garlic and fry for 5 minutes, until softened. Add the chicken pieces and fry for 5–10 minutes, until browned on all sides.

2 Pour in the wine and add the tomatoes with their juice, the sugar, cinnamon, cloves, allspice, and salt and pepper and bring to the boil. Cover the casserole and simmer for 45 minutes–1 hour, until the chicken is cooked through and the juices run clear when a skewer is inserted into the thickest part of the meat.

3 Meanwhile, cut the artichoke hearts in half. Add the artichokes and the olives to the casserole 10 minutes before the end of cooking, and continue to simmer until heated through. Serve hot.

LOUISIANA CHICKEN

Serves: 4

Prep: 15 mins

Cook: 1 hour 10 mins–1¼ hours

Ingredients

- 5 tbsp sunflower oil
- 4 chicken pieces
- 55 g/2 oz plain flour
- 1 onion, chopped
- 2 celery sticks, sliced
- 1 green pepper, deseeded and chopped
- 2 garlic cloves, finely chopped
- 2 tsp chopped fresh thyme
- 2 fresh red chillies, deseeded and finely chopped
- 400 g/14 oz canned chopped tomatoes
- 300 ml/10 fl oz chicken stock
- salt and pepper
- chopped fresh thyme, to garnish

Method

1. Heat the oil in a large, heavy-based saucepan or flameproof casserole. Add the chicken and cook over a medium heat, stirring, for 5–10 minutes, or until golden. Transfer the chicken to a plate with a slotted spoon.
2. Stir the flour into the oil and cook over a very low heat, stirring constantly, for 15 minutes, or until light golden. Do not let it burn. Add the onion, celery and green pepper and cook, stirring constantly, for 2 minutes. Add the garlic, thyme and chillies and cook, stirring, for 1 minute.
3. Stir in the tomatoes and their juices, then gradually stir in the stock. Return the chicken pieces to the saucepan, cover and simmer for 45 minutes, until the chicken is cooked through and the juices run clear when a skewer is inserted into the thickest part of the meat. Season with salt and pepper, transfer to warmed serving plates and serve immediately, garnished with a sprinkling of chopped thyme.

SPICED CHICKEN STEW

Serves: 6 **Prep: 20 mins** **Cook: 1 hour 25 mins–1½ hours**

Ingredients

- 1.8 kg/4 lb chicken pieces
- 2 tbsp paprika
- 2 tbsp olive oil
- 25 g/1 oz butter
- 450 g/1 lb onions, chopped
- 2 yellow peppers, deseeded and chopped
- 400 g/14 oz canned chopped tomatoes
- 225 ml/8 fl oz dry white wine
- 450 ml/16 fl oz chicken stock
- 1 tbsp Worcestershire sauce
- ½ tsp hot pepper sauce
- 1 tbsp finely chopped fresh flat-leaf parsley, plus extra to garnish
- 325 g/11½ oz canned sweetcorn kernels, drained
- 425 g/15 oz canned butter beans, drained and rinsed
- 2 tbsp plain flour
- 4 tbsp water
- salt

Method

1. Season the chicken pieces well with salt and dust with the paprika.
2. Heat the oil and butter in a flameproof casserole or large saucepan. Add the chicken pieces and cook over a medium heat, turning, for 10–15 minutes, or until browned all over. Transfer to a plate with a slotted spoon.
3. Add the onions and peppers to the casserole. Cook over a low heat, stirring occasionally, for 5 minutes, or until softened. Add the tomatoes, wine, stock, Worcestershire sauce, hot pepper sauce and parsley and bring to the boil, stirring. Return the chicken to the casserole, cover and simmer, stirring occasionally, for 30 minutes.
4. Add the sweetcorn and butter beans to the casserole, partially re-cover and simmer for a further 30 minutes, until the chicken is tender and the juices run clear when a skewer is inserted into the thickest part of the meat. Place the flour and water in a small bowl and mix to make a paste. Stir a ladleful of the cooking liquid into the paste, then stir the paste into the stew. Cook, stirring frequently, for a further 5 minutes. Garnish with parsley and serve immediately.

CHICKEN & BROCCOLI CASSEROLE

Serves: 4 **Prep: 20 mins** **Cook: 30–35 mins**

Ingredients

400 g/14 oz broccoli florets

40 g/1½ oz butter

1 onion, thinly sliced

350 g/12 oz skinless, boneless cooked chicken, cut into bite-sized chunks

100 g/3½ oz crème fraîche

200 ml/7 fl oz chicken stock

25 g/1 oz fresh white breadcrumbs

55 g/2 oz Gruyère or Emmenthal cheese, grated

salt and pepper

Method

1 Preheat the oven to 200°C/400°F/Gas Mark 6. Bring a saucepan of lightly salted water to the boil, add the broccoli and cook for 5 minutes until tender. Drain well.

2 Meanwhile, melt 25g/1 oz of the butter in a frying pan, add the onion and stir-fry over a medium heat for 3–4 minutes until soft.

3 Layer the broccoli, onion and chicken in a 1.5-litre/2¾-pint ovenproof dish and season well with salt and pepper. Pour over the crème fraîche and stock.

4 Melt the remaining butter in a small saucepan and stir in the breadcrumbs. Mix with the cheese and sprinkle over the dish.

5 Place the dish on a baking sheet in the preheated oven and bake for 20–25 minutes until heated through, golden brown and bubbling. Serve hot.

1
2
3

CHICKEN TRAY BAKE

Serves: 4 **Prep: 15 mins** **Cook: 45–55 mins**

Ingredients

4 chicken legs

2 tbsp olive oil

2 red peppers, deseeded and thickly sliced

1 large courgette, halved lengthways and thinly sliced

1 large onion, finely chopped

1 fennel bulb, thickly sliced lengthways

800 g/1 lb 12 oz canned chopped tomatoes

1 tbsp dried dill

1 tbsp balsamic vinegar

pinch of soft light brown sugar

salt and pepper

fresh crusty bread, to serve

Method

1. Preheat the oven to 190°C/375°F/Gas Mark 5. Leave the chicken legs whole or cut them into drumsticks and thighs.
2. Heat the oil in a frying pan. Add the chicken pieces, working in batches, if necessary, and fry for 5–7 minutes until golden brown. Remove from the pan and keep hot.
3. Pour off all but 2 tablespoons of the oil. Add the red peppers, courgette, onion and fennel and fry, stirring, for 3–5 minutes until the onion is soft. Stir in the tomatoes, dill, vinegar and sugar and season with salt and pepper.
4. Bring to the boil, stirring. Place the chicken pieces on a baking tray and pour the vegetables over. Cover tightly with foil, shiny side down.
5. Bake in the preheated oven for 30–35 minutes until the chicken is cooked through and the juices run clear when a skewer is inserted into the thickest part of the meat. Serve with crusty bread.

CHICKEN, PUMPKIN & CHORIZO CASSEROLE

Serves: 4 **Prep: 25 mins** **Cook: 1½ hours**

Ingredients

- 1 whole chicken, weighing 5 lb/2.25 kg cut into 8 pieces
- flour, for dusting
- 3 tbsp olive oil
- 200 g/7 oz fresh chorizo sausages, roughly sliced
- small bunch of sage leaves
- 1 onion, chopped
- 6 cloves garlic, sliced
- 2 sticks celery, sliced
- 1 small pumpkin/ butternut squash, peeled and roughly chopped
- 200 ml/7 fl oz dry sherry
- 600 ml/1 pint chicken stock
- 400 g/14 oz chopped tomatoes
- 2 bay leaves
- salt and pepper
- 1 tbsp chopped fresh flat-leaf parsley

Method

1. Preheat the oven to 180°C/350°F/Gas Mark 4.
2. Dust the chicken pieces in the flour. Fry the chicken in the olive oil in a casserole with the chorizo and sage leaves, until golden brown. Remove with a slotted spoon and reserve. You may need to do this in two batches.
3. Add the onion, garlic, celery and pumpkin to the casserole and cook for 20 minutes or until the mixture is golden brown.
4. Add the sherry, chicken stock, tomatoes and bay leaves, and season with salt and pepper.
5. Return the chicken, chorizo and sage to the casserole dish.
6. Cover with a lid and cook in the oven for 1 hour, until the chicken is cooked through and the juices run clear when a skewer is inserted into the thickest part of the meat.
7. Remove from the oven, discard the bay leaves, stir in the chopped parsley and serve.

★ Variation

Omit the pumpkin from the recipe and instead add two large, deseeded and sliced red peppers with the onion.

AROUND THE WORLD

COQ AU VIN 208
BAKED CHICKEN & CHORIZO PAELLA 210
CHICKEN MOLE POBLANO 212
SWEET & SOUR CHICKEN 214
CHICKEN GUMBO 216
HARISSA CHICKEN WITH CHICKPEA MASH 218
CHICKEN FRICASSÉE 219
GONG BAU CHICKEN 220
CHICKEN BURRITO BOWLS 222
CHICKEN KATSU 224
CHICKEN & MUSHROOM MARSALA 226
SPANISH-STYLE ROAST CHICKEN WITH POTATOES & SAUSAGE 228
CHICKEN TIKKA MASALA 229
YAKI SOBA 230
GREEN CHICKEN CURRY 231
CHICKEN TAGINE 232
CHICKEN PARMESAN 234
TERIYAKI CHICKEN 236
MINI CHIMICHANGAS 238
SPANISH CHICKEN WITH TOMATO & CHOCOLATE SAUCE 240
MOROCCAN-STYLE MINCE 242
CHICKEN & CHILLI ENCHILADAS 244
MEDITERRANEAN CHICKEN PARCELS 246
CHICKEN CACCIATORA 247
JAMBALAYA 248
CHICKEN RISOTTO WITH SAFFRON 250
THAI CHICKEN 252

COQ AU VIN

Serves: 4 **Prep: 15 mins** **Cook: 1 hour 20 mins**

Ingredients

- 55 g/2 oz butter
- 2 tbsp olive oil
- 1.8 kg/4 lb chicken pieces
- 115 g/4 oz rindless smoked bacon, cut into strips
- 115 g/4 oz baby onions
- 115 g/4 oz chestnut mushrooms, halved
- 2 garlic cloves, finely chopped
- 2 tbsp brandy
- 225 ml/8 fl oz red wine
- 300 ml/10 fl oz chicken stock
- 1 bouquet garni
- 2 tbsp plain flour
- salt and pepper
- bay leaves, to garnish

Method

1. Melt half the butter with the oil in a large flameproof casserole. Add the chicken and cook over a medium heat, stirring, for 8–10 minutes, or until browned all over. Add the bacon, onions, mushrooms and garlic.
2. Pour in the brandy and set it alight with a match or taper. When the flames have died down, add the wine, stock and bouquet garni and season to taste with salt and pepper. Bring to the boil, reduce the heat and simmer gently for 1 hour, until the chicken is cooked through and the juices run clear when a skewer is inserted into the thickest part of the meat.
3. Remove and discard the bouquet garni. Transfer the chicken to a large plate and keep warm. Mix the flour with the remaining butter and whisk the beurre manié into the casserole, a little at a time. Bring to the boil, return the chicken to the casserole and heat through. Garnish with bay leaves and serve immediately (do not eat the bay leaves).

★ Variation

Omit the chicken stock and use all red wine as the liquid for this casserole.

BAKED CHICKEN & CHORIZO PAELLA

Serves: 4 **Prep: 25 mins** **Cook: 40–45 mins**

Ingredients

- 2 tbsp olive oil
- 100 g/3½ oz chorizo sausages, skinned and sliced
- 1 onion, finely chopped
- 1 red pepper, deseeded and roughly chopped
- 400 g/14 oz skinless, boneless chicken thighs, chopped
- 4 large garlic cloves, finely chopped
- 350 g/12 oz paella rice
- 150 g/5½ oz frozen peas
- 1 tsp Spanish sweet paprika
- large pinch of saffron threads
- 125 ml/4 fl oz dry white wine
- 700 ml/1¼ pints chicken stock or vegetable stock
- 200 g/7 oz large raw prawns, peeled and deveined
- salt and pepper
- chopped fresh flat-leaf parsley, to garnish
- lemon wedges, to serve

Method

1. Preheat the oven to 220°C/425°F/Gas Mark 7. Heat the oil in a flameproof casserole over a high heat. Reduce the heat to medium–low, add the chorizo and fry, stirring, for 3–4 minutes until it starts to brown and gives off its oil. Remove from the pan and pour off all but 2 tablespoons of the oil.
2. Add the onion and red pepper and fry, stirring, for 3–5 minutes until soft. Add the chicken and garlic and stir until the chicken is coloured all over.
3. Add the rice and peas, gently stirring until the rice is coated in oil. Stir in the paprika and saffron threads, then add the wine and stock and season. Bring to the boil, stirring occasionally, then transfer to the preheated oven and bake, uncovered, for 15 minutes.
4. Remove from the oven and add the prawns and chorizo, pushing them down into the rice. Return to the oven and bake for a further 10 minutes, or until the rice is tender, the prawns are pink and cooked through, the chicken is cooked through and the juices run clear when a skewer is inserted into the thickest part of the meat. Garnish with parsley and serve with lemon wedges.

CHICKEN MOLE POBLANO

Serves: 4 **Prep: 25 mins** **Cook: 1½ hours**

Ingredients

- 3 tbsp olive oil
- 4 chicken pieces, about 175 g/6 oz each, halved
- 1 onion, chopped
- 2 garlic cloves, finely chopped
- 1 hot dried red chilli, reconstituted and finely chopped
- 1 tbsp sesame seeds, toasted, plus extra to garnish
- 1 tbsp chopped almonds
- ½ tsp each of ground cinnamon, cumin and cloves
- 3 tomatoes, peeled and chopped
- 2 tbsp raisins
- 350 ml/12 fl oz chicken stock
- 1 tbsp peanut butter
- 25 g/1 oz plain chocolate, grated, plus extra to garnish
- salt and pepper

Method

1. Heat the oil in a large frying pan. Add the chicken and cook until browned on all sides. Remove the chicken pieces with a slotted spoon and set aside.
2. Add the onion, garlic and chilli and cook for 5 minutes, or until softened. Add the sesame seeds, almonds and spices and cook, stirring, for 2 minutes. Add the tomatoes, raisins, stock, peanut butter and chocolate and stir well.
3. Season to taste with salt and pepper and simmer for 5 minutes. Transfer the mixture to a food processor and process until smooth (you may need to do this in batches). Return the mixture to the frying pan, add the chicken and bring to the boil. Reduce the heat, cover and simmer for 1 hour, until the chicken is cooked through and the juices run clear when a skewer is inserted into the thickest part of the meat.
4. Serve garnished with sesame seeds and a little grated chocolate.

SWEET & SOUR CHICKEN

Serves: 6 **Prep: 15 mins, plus marinating** **Cook: 15–20 mins**

Ingredients

450 g/1 lb skinless, boneless chicken breasts, diced
5 tbsp vegetable or groundnut oil
½ tsp crushed garlic
½ tsp finely chopped fresh ginger
1 green pepper, deseeded and roughly chopped
1 onion, roughly chopped
1 carrot, finely sliced
1 tsp sesame oil
1 tbsp finely chopped spring onion
cooked rice, to serve

Marinade

2 tsp light soy sauce
1 tsp Chinese rice wine
pinch of white pepper
pinch of salt
dash of sesame oil

Sauce

8 tbsp rice vinegar
4 tbsp sugar
2 tsp light soy sauce
6 tbsp tomato ketchup

Method

1. Cut the chicken into cubes and put in a dish. Combine the marinade ingredients and pour over the chicken. Leave to marinate for at least 20 minutes. Drain the chicken, discarding the marinade.
2. To make the sauce, heat the vinegar in a pan and add the sugar, soy sauce and tomato ketchup. Stir to dissolve the sugar, then set aside.
3. Heat a wok over a high heat, then add 3 tablespoons of the vegetable oil. Stir-fry the chicken until it starts to turn golden brown. Remove and set aside. Wipe out the wok with kitchen paper.
4. Heat the wok over a high heat, and add the remaining vegetable oil and cook the garlic and ginger until fragrant. Add the pepper, onion and carrot and cook for 2 minutes. Return the chicken to the wok and cook for 1 minute, or until cooked through. Add the sauce and sesame oil, then stir in the spring onion and serve immediately with freshly cooked rice.

1
2
4

CHICKEN GUMBO

Serves: 4–6

Prep: 35 mins, plus cooling

Cook: 2 hours–2 hours 5 mins

Ingredients

- 1 whole chicken, weighing 1.5 kg/3 lb 5 oz, cut into 6 pieces
- 2 celery sticks, 1 broken in half and 1 finely chopped
- 1 carrot, chopped
- 2 onions, 1 sliced and 1 chopped
- 2 bay leaves
- ¼ tsp salt
- 4 tbsp corn oil or groundnut oil
- 50 g/1¾ oz plain flour
- 2 large garlic cloves, crushed
- 1 green pepper, cored, deseeded and diced
- 450 g/1 lb fresh okra, trimmed, then cut crossways into 1-cm/½-inch slices
- 225 g/8 oz andouille sausage or Polish kielbasa, sliced
- 2 tbsp tomato purée
- 1 tsp dried thyme
- ½ tsp cayenne pepper
- ¼ tsp pepper
- 400 g/14 oz canned plum tomatoes
- cooked long-grain rice and hot pepper sauce, to serve

Method

1. Put the chicken into a large saucepan with water to cover, set over a medium–high heat and bring to the boil, skimming the surface to remove the foam. When the foam stops rising, reduce the heat to medium and add the celery stick halves, carrot, sliced onion, 1 bay leaf and salt. Simmer for 20 minutes, until the chicken is cooked through and the juices run clear when a skewer is inserted into the thickest part of the meat. Strain the chicken, reserving 1 litre/1¾ pints of the liquid. When the chicken is cool enough to handle, remove and discard the skin, bones and flavourings. Cut the flesh into bite-sized pieces and reserve.
2. Heat the oil in a large saucepan over a medium–high heat for 2 minutes. Reduce the heat to low, sprinkle in the flour and stir to make a roux. Stir constantly for 20 minutes, or until the roux turns hazelnut-brown. If black specks appear, it is burnt and you will have to start again.
3. Add the chopped celery, chopped onion, garlic, green pepper and okra to the saucepan. Increase the heat to medium–high and cook, stirring frequently, for 5 minutes. Add the sausage and cook, stirring frequently, for 2 minutes.

4 Stir in the remaining ingredients, including the second bay leaf and the reserved cooking liquid. Bring to the boil, crushing the tomatoes with a wooden spoon. Reduce the heat to low–medium and simmer, uncovered, for 30 minutes, stirring occasionally.

5 Add the chicken to the pan and simmer for a further 30 minutes. Taste and adjust the seasoning, if necessary. Remove and discard the bay leaves and spoon the gumbo over the rice. Serve with a bottle of hot pepper sauce on the side.

HARISSA CHICKEN WITH CHICKPEA MASH

Serves: 4

Prep: 20 mins, plus marinating

Cook: 20–30 mins

Ingredients

4 skinless, boneless chicken breasts

1 tbsp olive oil

8 tsp harissa (chilli) paste

salt and pepper

Chickpea mash

2 tbsp olive oil

2–3 garlic cloves, crushed

400 g/14 oz canned chickpeas, drained and rinsed

4 tbsp milk

3 tbsp chopped fresh coriander, plus extra to garnish

salt and pepper

Method

1. Make a few shallow slashes in each chicken breast. Place the chicken in a dish, brush with the oil and coat both sides with the harissa paste. Season well with salt and pepper, cover and leave to marinate in the refrigerator for 30 minutes.
2. Preheat the oven to 220°C/425°F/Gas Mark 7. Transfer the chicken breasts to a roasting tin and roast for about 20–30 minutes, until the chicken is cooked through and the juices run clear when a skewer is inserted into the thickest part of the meat.
3. Meanwhile, make the chickpea mash. Heat the oil in a saucepan and gently cook the garlic for 1 minute, then add the chickpeas and milk, and heat through for a few minutes. Transfer to a blender or food processor and purée until smooth. Season to taste with salt and pepper and stir in the coriander.
4. To serve, slice the chicken breasts. Divide the chickpea mash between four plates, top each with a sliced chicken breast and garnish with coriander.

CHICKEN FRICASSÉE

Serves: 4 **Prep: 15 mins** **Cook: 35–40 mins**

Ingredients

- 1 tbsp plain flour
- 4 skinless, boneless chicken breasts, diced
- 1 tbsp sunflower or corn oil
- 8 baby onions
- 2 garlic cloves, crushed
- 225 ml/8 fl oz chicken stock
- 2 carrots, diced
- 2 celery sticks, diced
- 225 g/8 oz frozen peas
- 1 yellow pepper, deseeded and diced
- 115 g/4 oz button mushrooms, sliced
- 125 ml/4 fl oz low-fat natural yogurt
- 3 tbsp chopped fresh parsley
- salt and white pepper

Method

1. Spread out the flour on a dish and season well with salt and white pepper. Add the chicken and, using your hands, coat in the flour.
2. Heat the oil in a heavy-based saucepan. Add the onions and garlic, and cook over a low heat, stirring occasionally, for 5 minutes. Add the chicken and cook, stirring, for 10 minutes, or until just beginning to colour.
3. Gradually stir in the stock, then add the carrots, celery and peas. Bring to the boil, then reduce the heat, cover and simmer for 5 minutes. Add the yellow pepper and the mushrooms, cover and simmer for a further 10 minutes until the chicken is cooked through.
4. Stir in the yogurt and parsley, and season to taste with salt and white pepper. Cook for 1–2 minutes, or until heated through, then transfer to plates and serve immediately.

GONG BAU CHICKEN

Serves: 4

Prep: 20 mins, plus marinating

Cook: 10–15 mins

Ingredients

2 skinless, boneless chicken breasts, diced

1 tbsp groundnut or vegetable oil

10 dried red chillies, or to taste, each snipped into 2–3 pieces

3 garlic cloves, finely sliced

2.5-cm/1-inch piece fresh ginger, finely sliced

1 tsp Sichuan peppercorns

1 tbsp finely chopped spring onion

85 g/3 oz roasted peanuts

cooked rice, to serve

Marinade

2 tsp light soy sauce

1 tsp Chinese rice wine

½ tsp sugar

Sauce

1 tsp light soy sauce

1 tsp dark soy sauce

1 tsp black rice vinegar

few drops of sesame oil

2 tbsp chicken stock

1 tsp sugar

Method

1 Combine the marinade ingredients and pour over the chicken. Leave to marinate for at least 20 minutes. Combine all the ingredients for the sauce and set aside.

2 Heat the wok over a medium–high heat, then add the groundnut oil. Stir-fry the chillies until crisp and fragrant. Add the chicken pieces and the marinade. When the chicken pieces begin to turn white, add the garlic, ginger, peppercorns and spring onion. Stir-fry for about 5 minutes, or until the chicken is cooked through.

3 Add the sauce to the wok and mix together thoroughly. Stir in the peanuts and serve immediately with freshly cooked rice.

1
2
2

CHICKEN BURRITO BOWLS

Serves: 4 **Prep: 25 mins** **Cook: 1¼ hours**

Ingredients

- 6 skinless chicken thighs
- 1 litre/1¾ pints water
- 400 g/14 oz canned chopped tomatoes
- 2 bay leaves
- 2 pickled Serrano or jalapeño chillies, chopped
- 2 limes, sliced
- 1 onion, halved
- 1 tbsp Mexican oregano
- 2 tsp ancho chilli powder
- 2 tsp ground coriander
- 2 tsp ground cumin
- 300 g/10½ oz easy-cook long-grain rice
- salt and pepper

To serve

- chopped fresh coriander
- 2 avocados, peeled, stoned, diced and tossed with lime juice
- other accompaniments of your choice, such as grated cheeses, pitted black olives, soured cream and chopped jalapeño peppers

Method

1. Put the chicken and water into a saucepan and slowly bring to the boil, skimming the surface as necessary. When the foam stops rising, stir in the tomatoes, bay leaves, chillies, lime slices, onion, oregano, chilli powder, ground coriander and cumin, and season to taste with salt and pepper. Adjust the heat so the liquid just bubbles, then leave to bubble for about 60 minutes until the liquid evaporates, the chicken is cooked through and the juices run clear when a skewer is inserted into the thickest part of the meat.
2. Meanwhile, cook the rice according to the packet instructions, then drain well and keep hot.
3. Use a slotted spoon to transfer the chicken to a bowl. Remove the bones and use 2 forks to shred the meat. Adjust the seasoning, if necessary.
4. To serve, divide the rice between four warmed bowls, then top with the shredded chicken. Sprinkle with chopped coriander and serve with the remaining accompaniments in small bowls for adding at the table.

CHICKEN KATSU

Serves: 4 **Prep: 30 mins** **Cook: 25–30 mins**

Ingredients

- 4 skinless, boneless chicken breasts, about 150 g/5½ oz each
- 3 tbsp plain flour
- ½ tsp salt
- ½ tsp pepper
- groundnut oil, for deep-frying
- 2 eggs, lightly beaten
- 100 g/3½ oz panko breadcrumbs
- cooked rice and green salad leaves, to serve

Curry sauce

- 4 shallots, chopped
- ½–1½ tsp dried chilli flakes
- 2 tsp curry powder
- 2 tsp garam masala
- 2 tsp clear honey
- 140 g/5 oz smooth peanut butter
- 1½ tbsp coconut or vegetable oil
- 225 ml/8 fl oz canned coconut milk
- juice of 1 lime
- 1½ tbsp ketjap manis (Indonesian soy sauce)

Method

1. To make the sauce, combine the shallots, chilli flakes, curry powder, garam masala, honey and peanut butter in the bowl of a food processor. Purée to a fairly smooth paste.
2. Preheat a wok over a high heat. Add the oil and heat until very hot. Add the spice paste and stir-fry over a medium heat for 2–3 minutes, until well mixed with the oil.
3. Stir in the coconut milk and simmer for 3 minutes. Stir in the lime juice and ketjap manis. Set aside and keep warm.
4. Halve the chicken breasts horizontally. Mix together the flour, salt and pepper and lightly coat each piece of chicken in the mixture.
5. Heat enough oil for deep-frying in a large wok to 180–190°C/350–375°F, or until a cube of bread browns in 30 seconds.
6. Put the beaten egg and the breadcrumbs into two separate wide, shallow bowls. When ready to fry, use tongs to dip the chicken in the beaten egg. Allow the excess egg to drip back into the bowl. Dip the chicken in the breadcrumbs, turning to coat.

7 Fry the chicken in two batches, cooking each batch for 5 minutes, turning halfway through, until the crumbs are golden, the chicken is cooked through and the juices run clear when a skewer is inserted into the thickest part of the meat.

8 Transfer to a board and slice each chicken piece. Arrange on individual warmed plates and pour over the sauce. Serve with freshly cooked rice and green salad leaves.

CHICKEN & MUSHROOM MARSALA

Serves: 4 **Prep: 20 mins** **Cook: 35–40 mins**

Ingredients

- 4 thick slices of Italian or French bread
- 1 garlic clove, halved
- 4 large boneless chicken breasts
- 2 tbsp olive oil, plus extra for brushing
- 8 large mushrooms, sliced
- 2 tbsp finely chopped shallot
- 1½ tbsp plain flour
- 350 ml/12 fl oz Marsala
- 450 ml/16 fl oz chicken stock
- 25 g/1 oz chilled butter, diced
- 1 tbsp chopped fresh parsley
- salt and pepper

Method

1. Preheat the grill. Lightly brush the bread slices with oil and toast under the preheated grill until golden brown on both sides. Rub the cut sides of the garlic clove over the toasted slices, then set aside. Finely chop the garlic.
2. Season the chicken breasts generously with salt and pepper. Heat the oil in a frying pan over a medium–high heat. Add the chicken, skin side down, and cook for 5 minutes, then turn over and cook for a further 5 minutes, until the chicken is cooked through and the juices run clear when a skewer is inserted into the thickest part of the meat. Remove from the pan and set aside.
3. Add the mushrooms and a pinch of salt to the pan, reduce the heat to medium and cook until the mushrooms are beginning to give up their juices. Continue to cook until all the liquid has evaporated and the mushrooms are beginning to brown. Add the shallot and garlic, and cook, stirring constantly, for 1 minute. Stir in the flour and cook, stirring, for 2 minutes.
4. Carefully pour in the Marsala, increase the heat to high and cook, stirring constantly, for 2 minutes. Pour in the stock, bring to the boil and cook until the sauce begins to reduce and thicken slightly.

Reduce the heat to very low, return the chicken to the pan and reheat gently.

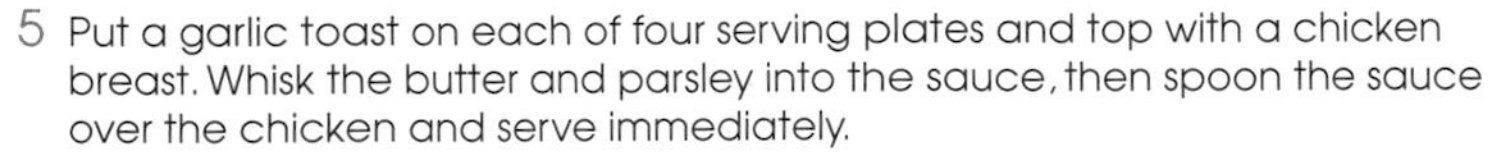

5 Put a garlic toast on each of four serving plates and top with a chicken breast. Whisk the butter and parsley into the sauce, then spoon the sauce over the chicken and serve immediately.

SPANISH-STYLE ROAST CHICKEN WITH POTATOES & SAUSAGE

Serves: 4–6

Prep: 20 mins

Cook: 1 hour 5 mins, plus standing

Ingredients

3 tbsp olive oil

1 whole chicken, cut into 8 pieces

1 large onion, roughly chopped

675 g/1 lb 8 oz small new potatoes, or larger ones cut into 5-cm/2-inch chunks

450 g/1 lb chorizo sausage, cut into 2.5-cm/1-inch pieces

1 tsp dried oregano

freshly grated orange zest

salt and pepper

Method

1. Preheat the oven to 190°C/375°F/Gas Mark 5.
2. Pour the oil into the base of a large roasting tin. Add the chicken, onion, potatoes, sausage, oregano and orange zest and rub everything with the oil. Season to taste with salt and pepper.
3. Roast in the preheated oven for 30 minutes, then remove from the oven and use a spatula to toss the chicken and potatoes in the orange-coloured fat released by the chorizo. Return to the oven and cook for about 35 minutes, or until the potatoes are tender, the chicken is cooked through and the juices run clear when a skewer is inserted into the thickest part of the meat. Leave to stand for 10 minutes before serving.

CHICKEN TIKKA MASALA

Serves: 4–6 **Prep: 15 mins** **Cook: 15–20 mins**

Ingredients

- 25 g/1 oz ghee or 2 tbsp vegetable or groundnut oil
- 1 large garlic clove, finely chopped
- 1 fresh red chilli, deseeded and chopped
- 2 tsp ground cumin
- 2 tsp paprika
- ½ tsp salt
- 400 g/14 oz canned chopped tomatoes
- 300 ml/10 fl oz double cream
- 8 pieces of cooked tandoori chicken
- pepper
- fresh coriander sprigs, to garnish
- cooked rice, to serve

Method

1. To make the tikka masala, heat the ghee, in a large frying pan with a lid, over a medium heat. Add the garlic and chilli, and stir-fry for 1 minute. Stir in the cumin, paprika, salt and pepper to taste, and continue stirring for about 30 seconds.
2. Stir the tomatoes and cream into the pan. Reduce the heat to low and leave the sauce to simmer, stirring frequently, for about 10 minutes, until it reduces and thickens.
3. Meanwhile, remove all the bones and any skin from the tandoori chicken pieces, then cut the meat into bite-sized pieces.
4. Add the chicken to the pan, cover and leave to simmer for 3–5 minutes, until the chicken is heated through. Garnish with coriander sprigs and serve immediately with rice.

YAKI SOBA

Serves: 2 **Prep: 15 mins** **Cook: 10–12 mins**

Ingredients

400 g/14 oz ramen noodles
1 onion, finely sliced
200 g/7 oz beansprouts
1 red pepper, deseeded and sliced
150 g/5½ oz skinless, boneless cooked chicken, chopped
12 cooked peeled prawns
1 tbsp oil, for stir-frying
2 tbsp shoyu
½ tbsp mirin
1 tsp sesame oil
1 tsp sesame seeds
2 spring onions, finely sliced

Method

1. Cook the noodles according to the packet instructions, drain well, and tip into a bowl.
2. Mix together the onion, beansprouts, red pepper, chicken and prawns in a bowl. Stir into the noodles. Meanwhile, preheat a wok over a high heat, add the oil and heat until very hot.
3. Add the noodle mixture and stir-fry for 4 minutes, or until heated through and the chicken is piping hot. Then add the shoyu, mirin and sesame oil and toss together.
4. Divide the noodles between two bowls.
5. Sprinkle with sesame seeds and spring onions and serve.

GREEN CHICKEN CURRY

Serves: 4 **Prep: 10 mins** **Cook: 15–20 mins**

Ingredients

2 tbsp groundnut or vegetable oil

4 spring onions, roughly chopped

2 tbsp green curry paste

700 ml/1 ¼ pints canned coconut milk

1 chicken stock cube

6 skinless, boneless chicken breasts, diced

large handful of fresh coriander, chopped

½ tsp salt

cooked rice, to serve

Method

1 Heat a wok over a medium–high heat, then add the oil. Add the spring onions and stir-fry for 30 seconds, or until starting to soften.

2 Add the curry paste, coconut milk and stock cube and bring gently to the boil, stirring occasionally.

3 Add the chicken, half the coriander and the salt and stir well. Reduce the heat and simmer gently for 8–10 minutes, or until the chicken is cooked through. Stir in the remaining coriander. Serve immediately with freshly cooked rice.

CHICKEN TAGINE

Serves: 4 **Prep: 20 mins** **Cook: 35–40 mins**

Ingredients

- 1 tbsp olive oil
- 1 onion, cut into small wedges
- 2–4 garlic cloves, sliced
- 450 g/1 lb skinless, boneless chicken breasts, diced
- 1 tsp ground cumin
- 2 cinnamon sticks, lightly bruised
- 1 tbsp plain wholemeal flour
- 225 g/8 oz aubergine, diced
- 1 red pepper, deseeded and chopped
- 85 g/3 oz button mushrooms, sliced
- 1 tbsp tomato purée
- 600 ml/1 pint chicken stock
- 280 g/10 oz canned chickpeas, drained and rinsed
- 55 g/2 oz ready-to-eat dried apricots, chopped
- salt and pepper
- fresh coriander leaves, to garnish

Method

1. Heat the oil in a large saucepan over a medium heat. Add the onion and garlic and cook, stirring frequently, for 3 minutes. Add the chicken and cook, stirring constantly, for a further 4 minutes, or until sealed on all sides. Add the cumin and cinnamon sticks and cook for a further minute.
2. Sprinkle in the flour and cook, stirring constantly, for 2 minutes.
3. Add the aubergine, red pepper and mushrooms, then cook, stirring constantly, for a further 2 minutes.
4. Blend the tomato purée with the stock, stir into the saucepan and bring to the boil. Reduce the heat and add the chickpeas and apricots. Cover and simmer for 15–20 minutes, or until the chicken is tender and cooked through.
5. Taste and adjust the seasoning, adding salt and pepper if needed. Garnish with coriander leaves and serve immediately.

★ Variation

For a spicy finish, stir in 2–3 teaspoons of harissa paste for the last 5 minutes of cooking.

CHICKEN PARMESAN

Serves: 4

Prep: 35 mins

Cook: 55 mins–1 hour, plus standing

Ingredients

100 g/3½ oz plain flour

2 eggs

200 g/7 oz dry breadcrumbs

4 skinless, boneless chicken breasts, 250 g/9 oz each

2 tbsp olive oil, plus extra if needed

250 g/9 oz mozzarella, sliced

125 g/4½ oz Parmesan cheese, grated

salt and pepper

chopped fresh flat-leaf parsley, to garnish

Simple marinara sauce

2 tbsp olive oil

1 large onion, chopped

2 large garlic cloves, chopped

1 tbsp dried mixed herbs

800 g/1 lb 12 oz canned chopped tomatoes

250 ml/9 fl oz passata

2 tsp dried oregano

pinch of sugar

Method

1 To make the sauce, heat the oil in a large saucepan. Add the onion and fry, stirring, for 2 minutes. Add the garlic and cook, stirring, until the onion is soft. Stir in the mixed herbs, tomatoes, passata, oregano and sugar and season to taste. Bring to the boil, then cover and simmer for 15 minutes. Transfer to a blender or food processor and purée.

2 Meanwhile, preheat the oven to 200°C/400°F/Gas Mark 6. Spread the flour over a plate. Beat the eggs in a wide bowl, and put the breadcrumbs on another plate. Halve the chicken breasts horizontally.

3 Place the chicken pieces between sheets of clingfilm and pound with a meat mallet or rolling pin until about 5 mm/¼ inch thick. Season both sides with salt and pepper. Dust a chicken breast with flour, shaking off the excess, then dip in the egg to coat. Dip in the breadcrumbs to coat both sides, then set aside and repeat with the remaining chicken pieces.

4 Heat the oil in a frying pan over a medium–high heat. Add as many chicken pieces as will fit in the pan in a single layer and fry on each side for 2 minutes, until the chicken is cooked through and the juices run clear when a skewer is

inserted into the thickest part of the meat. Fry the remaining pieces, adding extra oil, if necessary. Pour half of the sauce into a baking dish that will hold the chicken in a single layer. Arrange the chicken on top, then pour over the remaining sauce. Arrange the mozzarella on top and sprinkle over the Parmesan cheese. Bake in the preheated oven for 20–25 minutes, or until the cheese is melted, golden and bubbling. Leave to stand for 5 minutes, then garnish with parsley and serve immediately.

TERIYAKI CHICKEN

Serves: 4

Prep: 15 mins, plus marinating

Cook: 20 mins

Ingredients

4 boneless chicken breast

4 tbsp bottled teriyaki sauce, plus extra for brushing

peanut or corn oil, for brushing

Sesame noodles

250 g/9 oz dried thin buckwheat noodles

1 tbsp toasted sesame oil

2 tbsp sesame seeds, toasted

2 tbsp finely chopped fresh parsley

salt and pepper

Method

1. Using a sharp knife score each chicken breast diagonally across 3 times. Rub all over with teriyaki sauce. Set aside in the refrigerator to marinate for at least 10 minutes and up to 24 hours.
2. Cook the noodles in a saucepan of boiling water for 3–4 minutes until tender, or cook according to the packet instructions. Drain well and rinse in cold water.
3. Lightly brush the griddle pan with oil. Add the chicken breasts, skin side up, and brush again with a little extra teriyaki sauce.
4. Griddle the chicken breasts, brushing occasionally with extra teriyaki sauce, for 15 minutes, turning once, until the chicken is cooked through and the juices run clear when a skewer is inserted into the thickest part of the meat.
5. Meanwhile, heat a wok over a high heat. Add the sesame oil and heat until it shimmers. Add the noodles and stir round to heat through, then stir in the sesame seeds and parsley. Add salt and pepper to taste. Transfer the chicken breasts to plates and add a portion of noodles to each.

2
3
5

MINI CHIMICHANGAS

Serves: about 10 **Prep: 25 mins** **Cook: 35–45 mins**

Ingredients

- 2 tbsp vegetable oil, plus extra for frying
- 1 onion, finely chopped
- 250 g/9 oz fresh chicken mince
- 1 red chilli, deseeded and finely chopped
- 1 red pepper, deseeded and very finely chopped
- 100 g/3½ oz canned sweetcorn, drained
- 4 spring onions, trimmed and finely chopped
- 4 tbsp fresh tomato salsa
- 10 small flour tortillas
- salt and pepper

Method

1. Heat the 2 tablespoons of the oil in a non-stick frying pan, add the onion and mince and cook for 4–5 minutes, until the chicken starts to change colour and the onion is soft.
2. Add the chilli and red pepper and cook for a further 2–3 minutes until the chicken is cooked through. Remove from the heat and stir in the sweetcorn, spring onions, salsa, and salt and pepper to taste and place in a bowl. Wipe out the pan with kitchen paper.
3. Warm a tortilla briefly on each side in the pan. Place a large spoonful of the filling in the centre, fold in 2 sides of the tortilla, then the remaining 2 sides to form a small parcel. Secure with a wooden cocktail stick. Repeat with the remaining tortillas and filling.
4. Heat enough oil for frying in a frying pan. Add 2–3 chimichangas and cook for 2 minutes, then turn and cook for a further 2–3 minutes, until golden brown and cooked through. Drain on kitchen paper and keep warm while cooking the remaining chimichangas. Remove the cocktail sticks and serve.

SPANISH CHICKEN WITH TOMATO & CHOCOLATE SAUCE

Serves: 6 **Prep: 20 mins** **Cook: 1–1¼ hours**

Ingredients

6 chicken pieces

plain flour, for dusting

4 tbsp olive oil

Tomato & chocolate sauce

25 g/1 oz butter

2 tbsp olive oil

1 onion, finely chopped

2 garlic cloves, finely chopped

1 red pepper, deseeded and sliced

800 g/1 lb 12 oz canned chopped tomatoes

2 tbsp tomato purée

brown sugar, to taste

½ tsp ground nutmeg

½ tsp ground cinnamon

¼ tsp ground cloves

250 ml/9 fl oz dry white wine

70 g/2½ oz dark chocolate, finely chopped, plus extra grated chocolate to garnish

salt and pepper

Method

1 Dust the chicken portions with flour. Heat the oil in a large frying pan. Add the chicken, in batches if necessary, and cook over a medium heat, turning occasionally, for 8–10 minutes, until evenly browned. Remove the chicken from the pan and drain on kitchen paper.

2 Drain off the fat from the pan and wipe out with kitchen paper. To make the sauce, melt the butter with the oil in the same pan. Add the onion, garlic and red pepper and cook over a low heat, stirring occasionally, for 5 minutes, until softened. Stir in the tomatoes, tomato purée, sugar to taste, nutmeg, cinnamon, cloves and wine and season to taste with salt and pepper. Increase the heat to medium and bring to the boil.

3 Return the chicken to the pan, reduce the heat, cover and simmer for 20 minutes. Remove the lid from the pan and simmer for a further 20 minutes until the sauce has thickened and the chicken is cooked through and the juices run clear when a skewer is inserted into the thickest part of the meat. Add the chopped chocolate and stir constantly until it has melted. Garnish with grated chocolate and serve immediately.

MOROCCAN-STYLE MINCE

Serves: 4 **Prep: 15 mins** **Cook: 25–30 mins**

Ingredients

- 2 tbsp vegetable oil
- 1 large onion, finely chopped
- 2 garlic cloves, finely chopped
- 1 tbsp ground cumin
- 1 tsp ground cinnamon
- 2 tsp ground turmeric
- 500 g/1 lb 2 oz fresh chicken mince
- 500 ml/18 fl oz chicken stock
- 70 g/2½ oz raisins
- 250 g/9 oz couscous
- finely grated zest and juice of 1 lemon
- 25 g/1 oz toasted pine kernels
- salt and pepper
- sprigs of fresh flat-leaf parsley, to garnish

Method

1. Heat the oil in a large, non-stick frying pan, add the onion and cook over a low heat, stirring occasionally, for 4–5 minutes, until softened. Add the garlic and spices and cook for a further 1 minute over a medium heat.
2. Add the mince and cook, stirring frequently and breaking up the meat with a wooden spoon, for 4–5 minutes, until lightly browned. Add the stock and raisins, cover and cook over a low heat for a further 8–10 minutes.
3. Add the couscous, and salt and pepper to taste, stir and cover again. Simmer for 5–6 minutes, until the couscous has absorbed the stock and is fully cooked and the chicken is cooked through.
4. Remove from the heat, then stir in the lemon zest and juice and pine kernels. Garnish with parsley and serve immediately.

CHICKEN & CHILLI ENCHILADAS

Serves: 4 **Prep: 25 mins** **Cook: 35–40 mins**

Ingredients

- corn oil, for brushing
- 5 fresh hot green chillies, such as jalapeño, deseeded and chopped
- 1 Spanish onion, chopped
- 2 garlic cloves, chopped
- 2 tbsp chopped fresh coriander
- 2 tbsp lime juice
- 125 ml/4 fl oz chicken stock
- 2 beef tomatoes, peeled, deseeded and chopped
- pinch of sugar
- 350 g/12 oz skinless, boneless cooked chicken, shredded
- 85 g/3 oz Cheddar cheese, grated
- 2 tsp chopped fresh oregano
- 8 corn or flour tortillas
- salt

Method

1. Preheat the oven to 180°C/350°F/Gas Mark 4. Brush a large ovenproof dish with oil. Place two thirds of the chillies, the onion, garlic, coriander, lime juice, stock, tomatoes and sugar in a food processor and pulse to a purée. Scrape into a saucepan and simmer over a medium heat for 10 minutes, until thickened.
2. Mix together the remaining chillies, the chicken, 55 g/2 oz of the cheese and the oregano. Season to taste with salt and stir in half the sauce.
3. Heat a non-stick frying pan or griddle pan, then add the tortillas, one at a time, and warm for 10 seconds on each side. Divide the chicken mixture between the tortillas, spooning it along the centres, then roll up and place, seam side down, in the prepared dish.
4. Pour the remaining sauce over the enchiladas and sprinkle with the remaining cheese. Bake in the preheated oven for 20 minutes, until heated through and the cheese is golden and bubbling. Serve immediately.

MEDITERRANEAN CHICKEN PARCELS

Serves: 6 **Prep: 30 mins** **Cook: 30 mins**

Ingredients

1 tbsp olive oil

6 skinless, boneless chicken breasts

250 g/9 oz mozzarella cheese, sliced

500 g/1 lb 2 oz courgettes, sliced

6 large tomatoes, sliced

1 small bunch of fresh basil leaves, torn, plus extra to garnish

pepper

Method

1. Preheat the oven to 200°C/400°F/Gas Mark 6. Cut out six pieces of foil, each about 25 cm/10 inches square. Brush the foil squares lightly with the oil and set aside until required.
2. Using a sharp knife, make several slashes in each chicken breast, then place the mozzarella between the cuts in the chicken.
3. Divide the courgettes and tomatoes between the pieces of foil and season to taste with pepper. Scatter the torn basil over the vegetables in each parcel.
4. Place the chicken on top of each pile of vegetables, then wrap in the foil to enclose the chicken and vegetables, tucking in the ends.
5. Place on a baking sheet and bake in the preheated oven for about 30 minutes, until the chicken is cooked through and the juices run clear when a skewer is inserted into the thickest part of the meat.
6. To serve, unwrap the foil parcels and transfer the contents to warmed serving plates. Garnish with basil leaves and serve immediately.

CHICKEN CACCIATORA

Serves: 4 **Prep: 25 mins** **Cook: 55 mins**

Ingredients

1 chicken, weighing 1.5 kg/3 lb 5 oz, cut into 6 or 8 pieces

125 g/4½ oz plain flour

3 tbsp olive oil

150 ml/5 fl oz dry white wine

1 green pepper, deseeded and sliced

1 red pepper, deseeded and sliced

1 carrot, finely chopped

1 celery stick, finely chopped

1 garlic clove, crushed

200 g/7 oz canned chopped tomatoes

salt and pepper

fresh flat-leaf parsley sprigs, to garnish

Method

1 Lightly dust the chicken pieces with the flour. Heat the oil in a large frying pan. Add the chicken and cook over a medium heat until browned all over. Remove from the pan and set aside.

2 Drain off all but 2 tablespoons of the fat in the pan. Add the wine and simmer, stirring, for a few minutes. Stir in the peppers, carrot, celery and garlic, season to taste with salt and pepper and simmer for about 15 minutes.

3 Add the tomatoes and return the chicken to the pan. Cover and simmer, stirring frequently, for 30 minutes, until the chicken is cooked through and the juices run clear when a skewer is inserted into the thickest part of the meat.

4 Taste and adjust the seasoning, adding salt and pepper if needed. Transfer to bowls, garnish with parsley sprigs and serve immediately.

JAMBALAYA

Serves: 6 **Prep: 25 mins** **Cook: 35–45 mins**

Ingredients

- 2 tbsp vegetable oil
- 2 onions, roughly chopped
- 1 green pepper, deseeded and roughly chopped
- 2 celery sticks, roughly chopped
- 3 garlic cloves, finely chopped
- 2 tsp paprika
- 300 g/10½ oz skinless, boneless chicken breasts, chopped
- 100 g/3½ oz kabanos sausages, chopped
- 3 tomatoes, peeled and chopped
- 450 g/1 lb long-grain rice
- 850 ml/1½ pints chicken stock or fish stock
- 1 tsp dried oregano
- 2 bay leaves
- 12 large raw prawns, peeled and deveined
- 4 spring onions, finely chopped
- salt and pepper
- chopped fresh flat-leaf parsley, to garnish

Method

1. Heat the oil in a large frying pan over a low heat. Add the onions, green pepper, celery and garlic and cook for 8–10 minutes, until all the vegetables have softened. Stir in the paprika and cook for a further 30 seconds. Add the chicken and sausages and cook for 8–10 minutes, until lightly browned. Add the tomatoes and cook for 2–3 minutes, until they have collapsed.
2. Add the rice to the pan and stir well. Pour in the stock, oregano and bay leaves and stir well. Cover and simmer for 10 minutes.
3. Add the prawns and stir. Re-cover and cook for a further 6–8 minutes, until the rice is tender and the chicken and prawns are cooked through.
4. Stir in the spring onions and season to taste with salt and pepper. Remove and discard the bay leaves, garnish with parsley and serve immediately.

CHICKEN RISOTTO WITH SAFFRON

Serves: 4 **Prep: 15 mins** **Cook: 40 mins**

Ingredients

- 125 g/4½ oz butter
- 900 g/2 lb skinless, boneless chicken breasts, finely chopped
- 1 large onion, chopped
- 500 g/1 lb 2 oz risotto rice
- 150 ml/5 fl oz white wine
- 1 tsp crumbled saffron threads
- 1.3 litres/2¼ pints hot chicken stock
- 55 g/2 oz Parmesan cheese, grated
- salt and pepper

Method

1. Heat 55 g/2 oz of the butter in a deep saucepan. Add the chicken and onion and cook, stirring frequently, for 8 minutes, or until golden brown and cooked through.
2. Add the rice and mix to coat in the butter. Cook, stirring constantly, for 2–3 minutes, or until the grains are translucent.
3. Add the wine and cook, stirring constantly, for 1 minute, until reduced.
4. Mix the saffron with 4 tablespoons of the hot stock. Add the liquid to the rice and cook, stirring constantly, until it is absorbed.
5. Gradually add the remaining hot stock, a ladleful at a time. Add more liquid as the rice absorbs each addition. Cook, stirring, for 20 minutes, or until all the liquid is absorbed and the rice is creamy.
6. Remove from the heat and add the remaining butter. Mix well, then stir in the Parmesan cheese until it melts. Season to taste with salt and pepper. Spoon the risotto into warmed serving dishes and serve immediately.

THAI CHICKEN

Serves: 4

Prep: 15 mins, plus marinating

Cook: 20–25 mins

Ingredients

6 garlic cloves, roughly chopped

1 tsp pepper

8 chicken legs

1 tbsp Thai fish sauce

4 tbsp dark soy sauce

To garnish/serve

fresh ginger, cut into julienne strips

spring onions, sliced diagonally

fresh coriander sprigs

cooked rice

Method

1. Put the garlic in a mortar, add the pepper and pound to a paste with a pestle. Using a sharp knife, make a few diagonal slashes on both sides of the chicken legs.
2. Spread the garlic paste over the chicken legs and place them in a dish. Add the fish sauce and soy sauce and turn the chicken to coat well. Cover with clingfilm and leave to marinate in the refrigerator for 2 hours.
3. Preheat the grill. Reserving the marinade, drain the chicken legs. Put them on a grill rack and cook under the preheated grill, turning and basting frequently with the reserved marinade, for 20–25 minutes, until the chicken is cooked through and the juices run clear when a skewer is inserted into the thickest part of the meat.
4. Transfer the chicken to serving plates and garnish with ginger, spring onions and coriander sprigs. Serve immediately with rice.

★ Variation

Add some freshly grated lime zest to the garlic paste for a fresh and zingy flavour.

INDEX

anchovies
- Chicken Caesar Salad 54
- Mediterranean Pan Bagna 81

apples
- Cheddar & Apple-Stuffed Chicken Breasts 144
- Chicken & Apple Bites 74
- Chicken Waldorf Salad 48
- Creamy Chicken with Apples 112
- Curried Chicken Soup 29

apricots
- Chicken Tagine 232
- Chicken Thighs with Sweet-&-Sour Apricot Sauce 179

aubergines
- Chicken & Aubergine Layers Baked in Tomato Sauce 182–183
- Chicken Tagine 232

avocados
- Chicken, Avocado & Chipotle Soup 20
- Chicken, Bacon & Avocado Salad 42
- Chicken Tortilla Soup 28
- Cobb Salad 36
- Smoked Chicken & Cranberry Salad 52

bacon
- Bacon-Wrapped Chicken Burgers 116
- Chicken, Bacon & Avocado Salad 42
- Chicken Carbonara 154
- Chicken Sweetcorn Chowder 18
- Chicken Noodle Soup 10
- Cobb Salad 36
- Deep-Pan Chicken Feast Pizza 122
- Fried Chicken with Tomato & Bacon Sauce 152

barley
- Chicken & Barley Broth 31
- Winter Pot-Roast Chicken 160

beans & pulses
- Chicken & Barley Broth 31
- Chicken & Bean Soup 30
- Chicken & Lentil Soup 14
- Chicken Tagine 232
- Harissa Chicken with Chickpea Mash 218
- Spiced Chicken Stew 198
- White Chilli 147

beansprouts
- Chicken Chow Mein 80
- Chicken Ramen 22
- Yaki Soba 230

broccoli: Chicken & Broccoli Casserole 200

carrots
- Chicken & Dumplings 172–173
- Chicken & Thyme Soup 32
- Chicken Breasts Braised with Baby Vegetables 108
- Individual Chicken Pies 114–115
- Winter Pot-Roast Chicken 160

celery
- Chicken & Dumplings 172–173
- Chicken & Thyme Soup 32
- Chicken Salad Cups 47
- Chicken Waldorf Salad 48
- Curried Chicken Salad 46

cheese
- Cannelloni with Chicken & Ham 132
- Cheddar & Apple-Stuffed Chicken Breasts 144
- Chicken & Orzo Bake 190
- Chicken Carbonara 154
- Chicken Crostini 92
- Chicken Escalopes with Goat's Cheese Sauce 118
- Chicken Fettuccini Alfredo 134
- Chicken Lasagne 140
- Chicken Noodle Casserole 136
- Chicken Parmesan 234–235
- Chicken with Tomato Sauce & Melted Mozzarella 124
- Chicken-Loaded Potato Skins 60
- Chicken-Stuffed Squash 162
- Cobb Salad 36
- Deep-Pan Chicken Feast Pizza 122
- Mediterranean Chicken Parcels 246
- Pesto Chicken Pizza 78
- Quesadillas 119
- Quick Chicken Nachos 96
- Smoked Chicken & Ham Focaccia 104

Chicken Balls with Dipping Sauce 94
Chicken Kiev 131
Chicken with Forty Cloves of Garlic 166

chillies
- Chicken & Chilli Enchiladas 244
- Chicken, Avocado & Chipotle Soup 20
- Chilli Chicken Soup 26
- Chilli Verde Chicken Stew 194
- Gong Bau Chicken 220
- Jerk Chicken Skewers with Rice 86
- Minced Chicken Skewers 79
- Piri Piri Chicken 64

coconut
- Chicken Katsu 224–225
- Green Chicken Curry 231

courgettes
- Chicken & Bean Soup 30
- Chicken Tray Bake 202
- Mediterranean Chicken Parcels 246
- Smoked Chicken & Ham Focaccia 104

couscous: Moroccan-Style Mince 242
Crispy Chicken Fingers 129

eggs
- Chicken Carbonara 154
- Chicken Fried Rice 68
- Chicken, Mushroom & Herb Omelette 90
- Cobb Salad 36

French beans
- Chicken & Bean Soup 30
- Chicken & Pesto Salad 40–41
- Warm Chicken & Mango Salad 38

ginger
- Chicken Thighs with Barbecue Sauce 76
- Sticky Ginger & Soy Chicken Wings 70
- Thai Chicken Cakes 98

grapes
- Chicken Waldorf Salad 48
- Chicken Wraps 97
- Curried Chicken Salad 46
- Pasta & Chicken Medley 34

Greek Herb Roast Chicken 181

ham
- Cannelloni with Chicken & Ham 132
- Cheddar & Apple-Stuffed Chicken Breasts 144
- Chicken-Loaded Potato Skins 60
- Smoked Chicken & Ham Focaccia 104

leeks
- Chicken & Lentil Soup 14
- Chicken Casserole with a Herb Crust 176
- Cream of Chicken Soup 8
- Garlic Chicken with Leeks 69

lemons
- Chicken & Lemon Soup 24
- Lemon & Herb Roast Chicken with Watercress 164–165
- Risotto with Lemon Chicken 126–127

limes
- Chicken & Lime Tacos 72
- Sticky Lime Chicken 120

mangoes: Warm Chicken & Mango Salad 38

mushrooms
- Chicken & Lentil Soup 14
- Chicken & Mushroom Marsala 226–227
- Chicken & Mushroom Soup with Puff Pastry 16
- Chicken & Vegetable Bake 188
- Chicken Chow Mein 80
- Chicken Escalopes with Goat's Cheese Sauce 118
- Chicken Fricassée 219
- Chicken in Riesling 192–193
- Chicken in White Wine 169
- Chicken, Mushroom & Herb Omelette 90
- Chicken, Mushroom & Tarragon Pie 148
- Chicken Noodle Casserole 136
- Coq Au Vin 208
- Hunter's Chicken 168
- Individual Chicken Pies 114–115

mustard
- Chicken with Mustard Cream Sauce 102
- Honey & Mustard Chicken 82

noodles
Chicken Chow Mein 80
Chicken Noodle Casserole 136
Chicken Noodle Soup 10
Chicken Ramen 22
Teriyaki Chicken 236
nuts
Chicken in Tomato & Almond Sauce 170
Chicken Katsu 224–225
Chicken Mole Poblano 212
Chicken Salad Cups 47
Chicken Satay Skewers 66
Chicken Waldorf Salad 48
Curried Chicken Salad 46
Gong Bau Chicken 220
Warm Chicken & Mango Salad 38

okra
Chicken Gumbo 216–217
Spicy Aromatic Chicken 196
Oven-Fried Chicken Wings 58

parsnips
Chicken & Vegetable Bake 188
Chicken Casserole with a Herb Crust 176
Winter Pot-Roast Chicken 160
pasta
Cannelloni with Chicken & Ham 132
Chicken & Lemon Soup 24
Chicken & Orzo Bake 190
Chicken & Pesto Salad 40–41
Chicken & Thyme Soup 32
Chicken, Bacon & Avocado Salad 42
Chicken Carbonara 154
Chicken Fettuccini Alfredo 134
Chicken Lasagne 140
Chicken Meatball Pasta 130
Chicken Ravioli in Tarragon Broth 12–13
Chicken Rigatoni Bolognese 150
Fettuccine with Chicken & Basil Pesto 84
Honey & Chicken Pasta Salad 44
Pasta & Chicken Medley 34
pastry
Chicken & Mushroom Soup with Puff Pastry 16
Chicken, Mushrooms & Tarragon Pie 148
Individual Chicken Pies 114–115
peas
Chicken Breasts Braised with Baby Vegetables 108
Chicken Fricassée 219
Chicken Fried Rice 68
Chicken Noodle Casserole 136
Creamy Chicken Hash 88
Individual Chicken Pies 114–115
peppers
Chicken & Spicy Tomato Sauce Parcels 142
Chicken & Vegetable Bake 188
Chicken Cacciatora 247
Chicken Chow Mein 80
Chicken Faijitas 100
Chicken Tray Bake 202
Creamy Chicken Hash 88
Jerk Chicken Burgers 138
Spiced Chicken Stew 198
potatoes
Chicken-Loaded Potato Skins 60
Chicken Sweetcorn Chowder 18
Chilli Verde Chicken Stew 194
Roasted Chicken and Red Potatoes 178
Spanish Style Roast Chicken with Potatoes & Sausage 228
prawns
Baked Chicken & Chorizo Paella 210
Jambalaya 248
Yaki Soba 230

Red Chicken Salad 50
rice
Baked Chicken & Chorizo Paella 210
Chicken & Lime Tacos 72
Chicken & Vegetable Bake 188
Chicken Fried Rice 68
Chicken Risotto with Saffron 250
Jambalaya 248
Risotto with Lemon Chicken 126–127
Roast Chicken 110

sausages
Baked Chicken & Chorizo Paella 210
Chicken Gumbo 216–217
Chicken, Pumpkin & Chorizo Casserole 204
Jambalaya 248
Spanish-Style Roast Chicken with Potatoes & Sausage 228
Southern-Style Chicken Drumsticks 146
Spicy Chicken Pittas 62
spinach
Chicken Lasagne 140
Chicken Ramen 22
Chicken-Stuffed Squash 162
squash
Chicken, Pumpkin & Chorizo Casserole 204
Chicken-Stuffed Squash 162
Sweet & Sour Chicken 214
sweetcorn
Creamy Chicken Hash 88
Chicken Fried Rice 68
Chicken Ramen 22
Chicken Sweetcorn Chowder 18
Mini Chimichangas 238
Pesto Chicken Pizza 78
Spiced Chicken Stew 198

Thai Chicken 252
tomatoes
Cajun Chicken 186
Cannelloni with Chicken & Ham 132
Chicken & Aubergine Layers Baked in Tomato Sauce 182–183
Chicken & Bean Soup 30
Chicken & Orzo Bake 190
Chicken & Spicy Tomato Sauce Parcels 142
Chicken & Vegetable Bake 188
Chicken Burrito Bowls 222
Chicken Cacciatora 247
Chicken Crostini 92
Chicken Gumbo 216–217
Chicken in Tomato & Almond Sauce 170
Chicken Lasagne 140
Chicken Meatball Pasta 130
Chicken Parmesan 234–235
Chicken, Pumpkin & Chorizo Casserole 204
Chicken Rigatoni Bolognese 150
Chicken Tikka Masala 229
Chicken Tortilla Soup 28
Chicken Tray Bake 202
Chicken with Tomato & Cinnamon Sauce 180
Chicken with Tomato Sauce & Melted Mozzarella 124
Chilli Chicken Soup 26
Cobb Salad 36
Devilled Chicken 174–175
Fried Chicken with Tomato & Bacon Sauce 152
Honey & Chicken Pasta Salad 44
Hunter's Chicken 168
Louisiana Chicken 197
Mediterranean Chicken Parcels 246
Pesto Chicken Pizza 78
Rich Chicken Casserole 158
Spanish Chicken with Tomato & Chocolate Sauce 240
Spiced Chicken Stew 198
Spicy Aromatic Chicken 196
White Chilli 147
tortillas, tortilla chips
Chicken & Chilli Enchiladas 244
Chicken Fajitas 100
Chicken Quesadillas 119
Chicken Tortilla Soup 28
Chicken Wraps 97
Mini Chimichangas 238
Quick Chicken Nachos 96
turnips
Chicken & Barley Broth 31
Chicken Breasts Braised with Baby Vegetables 108

Ultimate Chicken Burger 128

Whole Roast Garlic Herb Chicken with Pan Gravy 184

This edition published by Parragon Books Ltd in 2014
LOVE FOOD is an imprint of Parragon Books Ltd

Parragon Books Ltd
Chartist House
15–17 Trim Street
Bath BA1 1HA, UK
www.parragon.com/lovefood

ISBN 978-1-4723-5997-1
Printed in China

New cover photography by Ian Garlick
Introduction by Anne Sheasby

Notes for the Reader
This book uses both metric and imperial measurements. Follow the same units of measurement throughout; do not mix metric and imperial. All spoon measurements are level: teaspoons are assumed to be 5 ml, and tablespoons are assumed to be 15 ml. Unless otherwise stated, milk is assumed to be full fat, eggs and individual vegetables are medium, and pepper is freshly ground black pepper. Unless otherwise stated, all root vegetables should be peeled prior to using.

Garnishes, decorations and serving suggestions are all optional and not necessarily included in the recipe ingredients or method. The times given are an approximate guide only. Preparation times differ according to the techniques used by different people and the cooking times may also vary from those given. Optional ingredients, variations or serving suggestions have not been included in the time calculations.

150 Recipes series